Evening with God

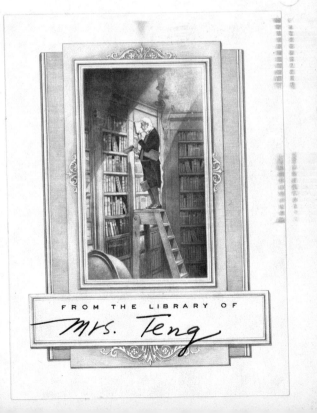

Evening with God

by
Paul Haschek

Thoughts and Prayers

*Translated
by
David Smith*

*Adapted
by
Dr. L. A. M. Gossens O.F.M.
and
A. Klamer*

Evening with God by Paul Haschek, translated by David Smith. Original German edition **Abend mit Gott** © Verlag Butzon & Bercker, Kevelaer. Translated from the Dutch edition **Avond met God,** edited by Dr. L. A. M. Goossens and Ds. A. Klamer, © 1976 Uitgeverij J. H. Gottmer, Haarlem. Copyright © 1979 Franciscan Herald Press, 1434 West 51st Street, Chicago, IL 60609. All rights reserved.

Library of Congress Cataloging in Publication Data

Haschek, Paul.
  Evening with God.

  Translation of Avond met God.
  1. Aged—Religious life. 2. Aged—Prayer-books and devotions. I. Goossens, Mathias. II. Klamer, A.
  BV4580.H2713   248'.3   78-15722
  ISBN 0-8199-0755-3

NIHIL OBSTAT:
  Mark Hegener O.F.M.
  Censor

IMPRIMATUR:
  † Msgr. Richard A. Rosemeyer, J. C. D.
  Vicar General, Archdiocese of Chicago

January 9, 1979

MADE IN THE UNITED STATES OF AMERICA

Pray without Ceasing

We have more time for prayer as we get older. When we were younger we always had so much to do and so many things to think of. Our time was so much more fully occupied.

Now life has become much quieter. We have time to reflect. Whether we choose to or not, we find that we have to place our innermost needs before God every day and, together with him, look for a solution to our problems.

For many of us, however, it is difficult to find the right words to describe our situation, express our gratitude, or make our longings known. Many of us have never really learned how to pray. We feel helpless and embarrassed when we try to address God. Our thoughts and feelings desert us. We need a definite idea that will touch off something inside us that will help us to pray.

The older we get, the more difficult prayer often seems to become. Sometimes it fails altogether and we feel barren and empty, tired and disappointed. We can say nothing. Our only comfort at such times is the knowledge that Jesus is always praying for us, that he is with us and in us, and that the Father hears his prayer.

All the same, it is most important to try to keep in touch with God as we get older. All our lives we are on the way toward God. That is why we should have already become intimate with God in prayer during our lives, before we reach the end — the fulfillment — toward which we are moving.

Prayer, however, is not simply repeating fine words. Prayer is life itself. It is responding to God. It is following Christ in the apparently insignificant moments when doing God's will has to be made a reality in the everyday events of our lives.

The thoughts contained in this book and the references to the situation in which older people find themselves are therefore not intended simply to provide a point of departure for prayer and reflection. They should also be used to help us live together with God.

In this way, the whole of life can become prayer, and we shall learn to pray without ceasing.

Dr. L. A. M. Goossens,

Chief Naval Chaplain, ret.

Rev. A. Klamer,

Ecumenical Radio Chaplain

VIII Trails, Endings and Beginnings 221

Contents

I. Time — Our Life

Make Use of the Time Given to You

The years of our life are three score and ten,
or even by reason of strength fourscore;
yet their span is but toil and trouble;
they are soon gone. . . .
So teach us to number our days
that we may gain a heart of wisdom.

Psalm 90:10, 12

Let us look at the question quite soberly. Sixty years come to about 525,960 hours. We sleep about 8 hours a day, or 175,320 hours in 60 years. 350,640 hours are therefore left to us for eating and the care of our bodies, work and relaxation, enjoyment and companionship, trouble and suffering, games and sport, study and prayer . . . and anything else that we do in life.

Our lives are measured in time. We make use of that time and then it is all over.

How much time is left to us? If we knew that we had only 1 year to live — 8,760 hours, of which we would spend about 2,920 hours sleeping — we would certainly make more careful use of the 5,840 hours left to us.

Our life is a gift, but it is also a task. We have to make something of it. It is given to us as an opportunity to go forward to meet God. When we were children, our parents cared for us. As adults, we devoted our time and energy to our fellow men and our work. Our life should end worthily, and if we do not take care of this ourselves, who will?

We should therefore have a good idea of what our life ought to look like after we have retired from work — and, what is more, prepare for this in good time. We should begin to adapt ourselves inwardly to this new phase in life before we reach it.

We have, it is true, a right to receive respect, help, and support from younger people, so that we can grow older with dignity and appreciation. But we also have the duty to recognize that we have fewer responsibilities than we did before we retired, that younger people have taken over our functions, and that what we have to say will not necessarily be very important simply because we happen to be older.

If we honestly admit that we are getting older, we shall at the same time recognize our need to deal consciously and responsibly with the problem of old age. We must also continue to be actively involved in contemporary society and its problems, even though we are much less directly responsible, and our concern must correspond to a real need and give us satisfaction.

We therefore need friends who understand us, partners with whom we have personal relationships, and acquaintances who share our interests. We must also have a positive attitude toward life and death, wisdom, experience, and a healthy way of life. We shall then be able to cope with the crises that come with old age.

No one automatically becomes deeply religious just because he is getting older. All of us, if we are to become really religious and learn how to pray deeply, need to practice prayer and we also need aids to prayer. We have also to be alert to what is required of us personally. The problems of old age cannot be solved simply by fine, pious sounding words. We need more than this — an answer that is close to the present needs of our heart. We have to find our way to God.

The quotations from Scripture and from mature, experienced authors, and the prayers and suggestions in this book are provided to help us to carry out our last important task in life in the right way. This final work is to end our lives worthily and prepare ourselves to meet God.

It is good to give thanks to the Lord,
to sing praises to thy name, O Most
High;
to declare thy steadfast love in the
morning

and thy faithfulness by night. . . .
For thou, O Lord, hast made me glad
by thy work;
at the works of thy hands I sing for joy.
How great are thy works, O Lord!
Thy thoughts are very deep!

Psalm 92:1-2, 4-5

Share what you can
and begin
with the limited possibilities
at your disposal:
this is trusting in God,
who can make wonders happen
through us.

Jan Beex

Thank You, Lord

When I look back at my life, I feel deep
   gratitude.
I thank you for all the good that you
   have done for me.
I thank you for all the happy times that I
   have experienced.

I thank you for all the times that I have
been successful;
they made me so happy.
I thank you for all the friendship that I
have been given;
it has enriched me so much.
I thank you for all the ways in which I
have been counseled;
I have learned so much from it.
I thank you for all the goodness that
has come my way.
I thank you for having been so close to
me so many times;
it has consoled me and renewed my
strength.
I thank you for being my God and for
loving me as I am.
The best way of thanking God for what
he gives us is to hand on his gift to
someone else.

Cardinal Faulhaber

I Need Your Help

I have often looked forward to being
old, but now that I am older it has
become a problem for me. I needed a
long life in order to acquire

experience, and now that I have it I find I can no longer get through on my own.

I need your help, Lord, in order to stay good and patient, to accept everything calmly and happily and to go forward to meet my fellow men lovingly and understandingly.

I have studied a great deal with the aim of turning it to good use one day. But I have forgotten so much. . . . And I don't know what to do with what I have left.

Simone de Beauvoir

As for man, his days are like grass;
he flourishes like a flower of the field;
for the wind passes over it and it is gone
and its place knows it no more.
But the steadfast love of the Lord is
from everlasting to everlasting
upon those who fear him
and his righteousness to children's children,

to those who keep his covenant and
remember to do his commandments.

Psalm 103:15-18

Stay with Me

Now that my life is restricted by old age and the troubles that go with it, I want my soul to be extended. But only you, the Lord of life, can fill my soul entirely. Come, then, into the center of my life and take your place there.

I want to make good use of my life as long as I am strong enough to do so. But only you, the Lord of glory, can give meaning and value to my efforts. Stay with me, then, and with your love make up for my deficiencies.

I am ready to endure the suffering that awaits me. It will enrich me and make me inwardly more mature. But only you, the God of patience, can give me strength to endure. Come, then, and make the end of my life happy and valuable.

I want to give meaning to my life by prayer and sacrifice, hope and trust,

love and faithfulness. But only you, the God of life, can entirely satisfy me and give my life total meaning. Come, then, and stay with me. I will then be rich enough and need nothing.

I want to enjoy life and I long for fulfillment in you. But only you, the God of blessedness, can satisfy my longing. Give me the certainty, then, that I will find completion in you.

Lead, kindly Light, amid the encircling gloom,
    Lead thou me on;
The night is dark and I am far from home;
    Lead thou me on.
Keep thou my feet; I do not ask to see
The distant scene; one step enough for me.

I was not ever thus, nor prayed that thou
    Shouldst lead me on;
I loved to choose and see my path; but now
    Lead thou me on.

I loved the garish day and, spite
of fears,
Pride ruled my will: remember not
past years.

So long thy power hath blest me, sure
it still
   Will lead me on,
O'er moor and fen, o'er crag and
torrent, till
   The night is gone,
And with the morn those angel faces
smile,
Which I have loved long since, and
lost a while.

Cardinal Newman

You Are Very Close to Us

You have given us life, the whole of
our life, as a task. Part of that task is to
become old meaningfully. The
fulfillment and completion of our task
in life is to abide in your love to the
end. We are helped in this task from
outside, but in the end we have to
make it a living truth quite alone.

Our greatest help, however, is your goodness and humanity. You became our brother. We thank you for this.

Abide in my love. If you keep my commandments, you will abide in my love, just as I have kept my Father's commandments and abide in his love. . . . This is my commandment, that you love one another as I have loved you. Greater love has no man than this, that a man lay down his life for his friends. You are my friends if you do what I command you.

John 15:9-10, 12-14

You Love Us

We ought to appreciate growing older because it indicates that you have loved us the whole of our long life. You have taken us seriously. You have given us talents. You have entrusted us with tasks.

You will ask us to give an account of ourselves, but you will also reward us. That is why you want us to take our growing older seriously.

We are still given time to put everything in order and even to add more to our store. Thank you for having loved us so much and for giving our life so much meaning even now.

Help us to make good use of the time left to us and to make each day valuable together with you. In this way, every day will also be valuable to us.

In giving form and content to our life, one of our most important tasks is to find ways and means of preventing ourselves from becoming rigid and from feeling alienated and lonely.

You Fulfill Our Life

Old age is relaxation after work, a period of rest that we have earned after carrying out our task in life. You want us to use this rest thoughtfully so that our life is given form and our contacts with our fellow men are meaningful.

Help us, then, to make this period of rest useful so that we benefit from it. Help us, too, to behave wisely and without prejudice toward others and always to be good and magnanimous. Let us also look forward with confidence to the fulfillment of our life in the hereafter.

Give our life content and meaning until the end.

The process of growing old is quite different from what most people think. It is not a withering away, but literally a process of growth. When you are old, you can be cheerful in a way which is usually impossible for younger people, and happy in a way that far transcends a youthful feeling of satisfaction.

Marcel Jouhandeau

You must hoist your sails
in the wind of infinity —
only then will you see the horizon
toward which you are sailing.

Alfred Delp

On the Way to You

Becoming old can be a burden. It brings difficulties, troubles, and anxieties. We have to learn how to accept illness and how to suffer. We have also to learn how to prevent ourselves from becoming spiritually dull. We have to accept the loss of our earlier skills and mobility.

Yet life goes on. For all of us, the biblical text holds good: *We must work while it is still day; when night comes no one can work* (see John 9:4).

All these difficulties and frustrations may also prevent us from going toward our eternal destiny calmly and in a spirit of recollection.

Lord, help us to find the right way.

The real problems of old age are nowadays not usually financial. The welfare state takes quite good care of us. There are residential homes for the elderly. Elevators are often provided. Specially designed wheel-chairs make us more mobile. We are in contact with the outside world through radio and television. There are clubs and associations that keep us in touch with other people.

No, the real problems are spiritual. We tend to feel inwardly empty, lonely, helpless, and useless. We feel neglected, unwanted, and at the mercy of powers that we do not understand.

Becoming old in the right way is often a greater achievement than anything else that we have been asked to do throughout our life.

Lord, help us find the right way.

Do not be anxious about your life, what you shall eat or what you shall drink, nor about your body, what you shall put on. Is not life more than food and the body more than clothing?

Look at the birds of the air; they neither sow nor reap nor gather into barns. Yet your heavenly Father feeds them.

Are you not of more value than they?

Matthew 6:25-26

O certain knowledge that salvation is there
and that there is only one mile between you and me!
Your vessel is still too far for me to hail it,
but I know that it is sailing toward me.

William of Merode

The Value of Old Age

You, Lord, have not made the value of old age dependent on our attitude toward it. We can always make our life valuable by loving and having something to spare for other people. This is the legacy that we can leave behind us. Help us, then, to recognize our task and to carry it out gladly and without anxiety.

Difficult people can often change and become better when they meet someone who is sympathetic and believes in them.

Paschasius of Marvilde

Do not lay up for yourselves treasures on earth, where moth and worm consume and where thieves break in and steal, but lay up for yourselves treasures in heaven. . . . Where your treasure is, there will your heart be also.

Matthew 6:19-21

What matters is not how old you are, but how you are old. Old age is a gift and a task. It is also a blessing that you have to accept thankfully and a burden that you have to bear courageously.

You should therefore not think of old age as something that you cannot escape. You should regard it rather as something that you are given to do something with.

Alois Stiefvater

II. All the Days of My Life

A Day for You

Lord, you have given this new day to me and with another little piece of my life.

Thank you for letting me go on living, for having created me, for having redeemed me through your Son and for having called me to your kingdom.

Thank you for having given me everything that I need, to go on living and enjoying my life.

Thank you for always thinking of me and loving me.

I dedicate this day to you. I offer you today all that I think and do, my work and my difficulties, everything that I enjoy and everything that I find hard.

Bless me. Let every thing that I do today please you and be a small act of homage to you.

I trust you, because everything that comes from you is good.

I want to belong to you, now and for ever.

The night is far gone, the day is at hand. Let us then cast off the works of darkness and put on the armor of light. Let us conduct ourselves becomingly as in the day, not in reveling and drunkenness, not in debauchery and licentiousness, not in quarreling and jealousy. But put on the Lord Jesus Christ.

Romans 13:12-14

Give my life today form and direction by your nearness to me. I promise to direct all my thoughts and feelings toward you. This will make my life meaningful.

If you look closely, very few people live in the present. Most of them intend to begin living shortly.

Jonathan Swift

If you keep God in sight, you will have a clear view of man.

I looked for my soul,
  but could not see it.
I looked for my God,
  but he escaped me.
I looked for my brother,
  and found all three.

In Your Hands

Father in heaven, you give me life
again with this new day. Thank you.
This gift makes me happy, because it
shows me that you love me. I feel
secure in your hands.

I offer myself to you today.
Whatever this day may bring, you will
help me. I want to please you in
everything I do, say, and think. In
everything that I have to bear today, I
shall think of the suffering of Christ
and you will bless it and make it
fruitful. If life is difficult for me today,
strengthen me so that I do not become
touchy or impatient.

Bless my family and friends and
help them in their work. Lead them on
the way to salvation.

Let me be happy today. Let me do something good today and bring a little happiness to others.

God gives every bird something to eat, but he does not put it into its nest.

Do your best and God will do the rest.

Every Day Another Task

With every day that you give me, you give me another task. As long as I live, there is always a task for me. I can do something good. I can pray.
I want to encounter you today in everything that I come across. In everything that happens to me you let me know what you want of me. Every opportunity to do something good, every person I meet, and everything that I have to suffer — they all tell me something about you.

Help me, Lord, to see you in all this experience and to serve you gladly.

People no longer have any time to see things properly. They have no time because they have no love. Love and time belong together.

Max Picard.

Everything we do has as much value as it has derived from our morning prayer.

St. Vincent de Paul

Lord, you live among us, but we do not recognize you. Help me to perceive and do your will. My life will then be better and happier.

Regard each day as a life in itself.

Seneca

Teach me how to be ready for you each day — how to do your will and live for you all through the day.

If you love life, make good use of time; your life consists of time.

Benjamin Franklin

Art is for me a form of religion. I can spend hours in God's creation. I receive it into myself and let it have its effect on me, with the aim of understanding its nature and character. Then I take a pencil and brush and reproduce it as its Creator made it. The most important element is to be at one with God. Faithful reproduction of nature is secondary. I glow with happiness when I do this.

Queen Wilhelmina

My Life Is Your Gift

You have given me life and have kept me alive until now. You have held me in your hands since my earliest youth and have never forgotten me even now, when I am old. The whole of my life is in your hands. That is why I shall go on entrusting myself to your love and grace.

Make me happy, even now, when I am no longer able to do very much. Keep me young in heart and cheerful until I can see your face.

We feel wonderfully protected by good powers. Comforted, we wait for whatever may come. God is with us in the evening and in the morning and quite certainly every new day.

Dietrich Bonhoeffer

God My Refuge

In thee, O Lord, do I take refuge;
  let me never be put to shame. . . .
Be thou to me a rock of refuge,
  a strong fortress, to save me.
For thou, O Lord, art my hope,
  my trust, O Lord, from my youth. . . .
Do not cast me off in the time of
  old age; forsake me not when my
  strength is spent. . . .
O God, from my youth thou hast taught
  me and I still proclaim thy wondrous
  deeds.
So even to old age and gray hairs,
  O God, do not forsake me,
  till I proclaim thy might
  to all the generations to come. . . .
O God, who is like thee?

Psalm 71

Full of happiness that you are my Father, I come to you today. Bless me throughout the whole of the day and let me experience your goodness and affection. You keep me alive.

I love you deeply. Give me your blessing today when I am working and if I enjoy anything. Help me if anything proves too much for me. Protect me against all disaster. Help me to be better, more pious, and more complete.

You have given me years during which I have been able to carry out my task in life. Help me now. Give me wisdom and patience so that I do not pride myself on what I have done. Let me rather be ready with love and with all my heart for the people who come after me.

Let me be glad that I have been able to do my life's work. Even though much of it is forgotten, the intention was honorable.

Even what you had given me for a little while was a sign of your love. And even though what you gave me then is in the past, you are still the same. You give out of goodness and you take out of goodness.

Even now I offer what I can still do to you. I trust entirely in your love.

It is easier to be a hero for a minute or an hour than quietly to live an ordinary life. Do just that — live a gray, monotonous ordinary life. The heroic aspect of it passes unnoticed. No one appreciates you for it. No one is interested in it. The person who has to go on living that gray, ordinary life and who still remains human is a real hero.

Fyodor Dostoyevski

Let my longing be calmed down today and transformed into true happiness by the people you have placed in my way today and by the knowledge that you love me.

It is a wise man who does not mourn for the things that he does not have, but is happy with what he has.

Epictetus

Watch out every day for something eternal, something that death cannot take away from you, something that will make both death and life more precious to you every day.

J. K. Lavater

O Lord, I place in your hands today,
although it is of little value,
all that I am,
all that I know,
all that I have on earth.

From now on,
for you and your greater glory,
as you require it
and otherwise not,
I will do or do without.

Lodewijk Makeblijde

I Dedicate Everything to You

I am interested in so many things. Sometimes I am quite enthusiastic. But when I am required to show real love to one of my fellow men, I often lack affection and warmth.

Let me gain some insight into the complexities of life and recognize your will. Give me the strength to serve my fellow men with all my heart. Give me the courage to do everything you want me to do.

I dedicate everything that I shall do today to you. Accept it as a gift from me.

Very many people have lost their faith in God because they have lost their faith in their fellow men — in the humanity of their fellow men. And many people have rediscovered their faith in God because they have met a good person, someone who has been able to take the bitterness — the cutting edge of his misery — out of his heart, perhaps when he was old or in a hospital.

Cardinal Faulhaber

I will approach the — apparently — so unimportant people whom I shall meet today with respect and love, because I encounter you in them. Help me, then, to love all people without restraint.

You have entrusted to us and to our
love those people who find life difficult
in our society. Let me be concerned
for them in your name. Give me
patience to do this and make me ready
to serve them properly.

Real love begins where nothing is
expected in return.

Antoine de Saint-Exupéry

Lord, I accept
this day
and all that it will bring
from your hands.
You are the way,
the truth and the life.
You are the way
that I want to go,
the truth
that I want to see,
the life
that will bear me up.
Coolness and fire,
sorrow and happiness —
everything is good
as it comes.

V. With Each Other and for Each Other 145

VI. The Day Is Drawing to a Close 187

Grant that it will be good.
  I begin this day
in your name.
Amen.

Ignaz Klug

You have created this day as something new. Let me break away from all outdated forms. Keep my heart young and full of life. All that I think and say and all my prayer and work must be a way to you.

Make Me More Mature

The older I get, the further I become separated from my fellow men. I can no longer go out as I used to. I cannot even understand everything any more. I am often regarded as old-fashioned. And not many of the people who used to understand me and whom I understood are still alive.

  Help me, Lord, at least to understand you. You know me better than anyone else and you know that my intention is good. I would like to

spend my days in such a way that I
find my fulfillment in you.

Let me therefore remain faithful in
small things. Let me wait patiently, full
of trust and faith. Let me be kind in my
judgments and happy with what you
still give me in your love.

When I finally leave the world,
receive me in your love.

What we do today is decisive for the
world of tomorrow.

Boris Pasternak

A person's wage is not what he earns
with his money, but what becomes by
it.

John Ruskin

*Which of you by being anxious can add
one cubit to his span of life?*

Matthew 6:27

We ask you, Lord, suggest to us what
we ought to do and be with us when

we do it. Then all our prayer and work will begin with you and be completed by you.

Give Me Strength

Even though I cannot do anything really great, I offer you everything that the day may bring — the little things that I do, the efforts that I make, my difficulties and my sacrifices.

If one has nothing particular to do, all kinds of things soon become less interesting. One feels lonely and neglected. One becomes more conscious of the hardness of life and its little discomforts. I offer all this to you as a sacrifice.

Everything that I am still able to do I want to do gladly. I want to exert myself to help other people and make them happy. Help me to do this, Lord.

It is full time now to wake from sleep. For salvation is nearer to us now than we first believed.

Romans 13:11

When I was looking for you alone and loved you only, I found myself and at the same time found you.

Thomas à Kempis

You Have Given Me Time

What would have happened to me if you had called me to leave this world years ago? Then I was in the prime of life. I was preoccupied with my work, at the mercy of my emotions and enslaved to all kinds of habits.

But you gave me many more years and the time to make up for everything that I had neglected or done wrong and to set my affairs in order. I thank you for this, Lord, every day.

Life is short, but it is of infinite value, because in it is hidden the seed of eternity. Happy is the man who understands the meaning of this truth.

Francis de Sales

Let me, Lord, forgo what is not necessary today and let the time that is saved be used to benefit those in need.

Not everyone who says to me "Lord, Lord" shall enter the kingdom of heaven, but he who does the will of my Father who is in heaven.

Matthew 7:21

A Moment of Grace

As long as I go on living, you give me again and again a moment that is "now" for me.

Let me not live exclusively in the past. Let me rather be ready to make use of the moment that is to come and to fill the time with worthwhile things.

What I do in all those moments that you give me has an indelible effect, even in eternity. Help me, then, to direct everything that happens to me now toward eternal life and to let it bear witness to your love.

Let me value each hour as a precious gift of your grace. Let me make use of every opportunity, and may everything that I do here on earth lead to eternal salvation.

As long as I live, Lord, you are the one who makes my life valuable. I thank you for this.

Carry God about with you in your life, then your life will carry you to God.

Margarethe Seemann

Through faith, Lord, fill me with joy and peace. Then, in your strength, I shall be able to do what is required of me today and do it happily.

When you serve the sick, remember that you are serving Christ.

Jan van Ruysbroeck

When the eternal sun, Christ, shines into the open heart, he makes that heart and all its inner forces grow and blossom and overflow with joyful sweetness. Then the wise man must behave like the bee. He must, with discrimination and forethought, fly to the gifts — to all the sweetness that he has ever felt, to all the good that God has ever done for him — and taste with the sharp point of love and with inner discernment. He should not, however, remain on one flower — on one of the gifts — but, laden with thanks and praise, fly back to the unity in which he wants to stay with God in eternity.

Jan van Ruysbroeck

III. Remaining Human

Abundant Life

You have given me life and have given it to me abundantly.

You come to seek out and to save what was lost and you chose me.

You are the good shepherd who lays his life down for his sheep, and you have redeemed me.

My life has been valuable only because you have blessed it. All the external success that I have ever had has been pleasant only because I have experienced inner joy from you. All that I have done has been worthwhile only because you have accepted it.

I ask you to go on being the content of my life.

If we reflect about our lives, what ought to surprise us most of all is the fact that we are alive.

Reinhold Schneider

Lord, I do not ask you for wealth or knowledge, but for your love. Only that can fill my life. Give me back the first tender love of my early days. Then the end of my life will be filled by you. Give me back the enthusiasm of my youth. Then my old age will be blessed.

What is man that thou art mindful of him, the son of man that thou dost care for him?

Thou hast made him little less than a god and hast crowned him with glory and honor.

Thou hast given him dominion over the works of thy hands and hast put all things under his feet.

Psalm 8:4-6

I Am a Human Being

I am a human being, your creature, the work of your hands.

My greatness and the nobility of my existence consist of that.

You, God, are there for me.

My life is founded on your grace.

I was created in your image and likeness.
I was begotten forever by your love.
What more can I ask?
It makes me thankful and glad.

Put on the new nature, created after the likeness of God in true righteousness and holiness.

Ephesians 4:24

At the beginning of every genuinely Christian life there is always a deep longing to be made new in Christ and an inner readiness to cast off the old man and to become fundamentally different.

Dietrich von Hildebrand

One of the marks of our society that sets such store by achievement is that anyone — however important his function or status — can be replaced very quickly. As soon as he is no longer active and influential in his work, his colleagues at once forget him. He is also very quickly forgotten in life as a whole. His achievements — of which he was so proud — disappear without a trace.

It is understandable and even necessary that we should be so easily and rapidly replaceable in modern technological society, because almost every form of work can be identified with a single function and this has to continue without interruption. What is distinctively human plays hardly any part in the functional society. Anyone who exercises a function can always be replaced by another, who may perform the same function even better.

If everything is judged according to its utility here and now, men and women may also be judged in the same way. This process can take place imperceptibly and we have to accept it with resignation.

You are clever only if you are human as well.

Jean Anouilh

A Wonderful Creation

I have received my body from you. It is a wonderful creation. All the forces and skills of my body, your creation, help me to serve you.

Help me to stay fit and well in body and soul. Then I will be happy and always capable of loving my fellow men deeply.

Live in my heart. Then I shall be your temple and I shall find my fulfillment in you.

Do you not know that your body is a temple of the Holy Spirit within you, which you have from God? You are not your own; you were bought at a price. So glorify God in your body.

1 Corinthians 6:19-20

As soon as you cease to look at myself critically, you are criticized by others — radically and destructively. You should not view old age in the light of such norms as health and declining abilities, but as a possible way of

becoming more mature. The older
person should place in the center of
his life something in which he is failing
— his ability to achieve. He should
become more mature and wise. He
can go on doing that until he dies.

Paul Tillich

Made Valuable by You

We are made valuable, not just by
what we achieve but by you. We have
inner wealth and beauty, and these
are valuable because you have
created and redeemed us and have
called us to glory.

Our present experience may
perhaps no longer be appreciated, but
the witness that we have borne
through our faith throughout our life
remains valuable for you. You value
our having held out despite all the
times that we have been put to the
test.

My life will remain valuable so long
as I rate spiritual values highly and am
faithful to the end.

It is healthy to reflect about what compels us to step outside ourselves.

Simone Weil

How highly do you value God? You will know this when you think about what he has become for you.

St. Bernard of Clairvaux

If, then, you have been raised with Christ, seek the things that are above, where Christ is, seated at the right hand of God. Set your minds on things that are above, not on things that are on earth.

Colossians 3:1-2

For You, Love Counts

When we were younger, our value was measured according to our physical strength and our skills. Could we think quickly and act intelligently? Were we economically productive? Were we influential? Could we contribute to society?

But what does all that mean if our life is without content? For love, what counts above all is a loving heart.

Give us, Lord, the strength and the opportunity to achieve something now in the service of our fellow men.

You, Lord, are life; your life is love and your love is an inexhaustible source of happiness.

Every morning that you give us, then, my soul ought to be glad because of you. Every night, when I close my eyes, my heart should once again entrust itself to you.

Complete in me what you have begun. Protect me and never leave me. Your goodness is more to me than life itself.

J. K. Lavater

Sustain My Strength

Sustain my health — it is such a great blessing. Leave me still a little strength, even if everything else leaves me. Even if I become slower and less agile, I would like still to be able to do something.

Sustain the health of my body and my soul. Let me be zealous in doing good.

How is your health? I ask you above all to care constantly for your body. The soul looks out through your eyes. If they are dim, the whole world is full of rain.

Goethe

Let me recognize you, as a real Christian should, as my Father and my God, whatever situation I may find myself in. However much my situation may change, you, Lord, remain the same.

You do not change, but I am subject to constant change. You are good, both when life is bad for me and I am put to the test and when you show me your favor and comfort me.

Blaise Pascal

Lord, I stand here before you. You made me — make me new. Let all my strength be put to your service. Let everything that I do today be good.

Let everything that happens today please you, so that, this evening, you will be able to say, as you did on the evening of each day of creation: It is good.

Romano Guardini

Healthy and well disposed —
that is true wealth.

Thank You for My Intelligence

I thank you, Lord, for my intelligence, which enables me to understand the world, distinguish the truth, and make use of the forces of nature. Thank you also for making it possible for me, through my intelligence, to understand and love my fellow men and also to find my way to you.

I also thank you, Lord, for all the good things that I am able to experience — books and music, the truth that gives meaning to my life, all the good that I have ever seen and done, every word that tells me something about you, every impulse in which you are active within me.

I thank you because you are the truth and, in you, I find the aim and purpose of my existence.

Let me know you better, Lord, and love you more. Let me have a happy experience of you. Strengthen me every day and increase my longing for the fulfillment toward which I am always moving.

Give me insight here — let that insight be perfect there. Give me love here — let that love be mature there. Give me joyous hope here — let me be happy there in union with you.

Anselm

We cannot always find something really great to do on our way through life. But there are small opportunities every hour for us to do something well and indeed very well — that is, with great love. For example, we can endure another person's bad mood....

It is much more beneficial for us than we usually think to overcome our own inclinations again and again.

St. Francis of Assisi

The thinker's task is to understand the world around him and to tell us how man ought to behave in life.

Oswald Spengler

Sustain My Spirit

Sustain my spirit, Lord, as I gradually decline physically. Give those who are looking after me, or will be looking after me, love, patience, and the strength to carry on.

Low spirits and depression — I do not want to suffer from these as I get older. Give me the strength to carry on cheerfully if things become difficult.

Let all the questions that trouble me and all the problems that concern me give way to the one great factor: how I shall appear in your presence.

Make it possible for many people to understand, Lord, what a great blessing it is to stay spiritually in heaven in the midst of so many transitory and foolish things in this world and to say, full of trust: Everything that troubles and saddens us will pass. It will pass, Lord, and we will go forward gladly toward a much richer kingdom.

Christoph Blumhardt

Remaining Spiritually Open

Experience costs a great deal. I have often had to pay a lot for it; it has cost me time and effort as well as money. What a painful, difficult process it is to become wiser and more under-standing, to learn how to avoid making mistakes and do good.

If I am to grow in experience of this kind, Lord, it is most important for you to stay at the center of my life and for me to remain open to what you say. I must learn to listen to you and only to you. Do not let me be satisfied with the latest news. Help me to remain spiritually open to everything that is happening around me and to see behind it. The only worthwhile activity is to serve you.

O the sweet and wonderful restlessness of the human heart! Always be restless, my soul, and feel uncomfortable in this world, until you have found your way to the refreshing source of immortal life — God himself, the most holy one. He alone can change your restlessness into peace. He alone can completely satisfy your longing.

St. Francis de Sales

The great things in life come only to people who pray.

Peter Wust

You Bring Fulfillment

I want to go on thinking about the spiritual background to old age. If I do this, I will be able to understand the positive values of being old: experience and wisdom, suffering and self-surrender, prayer and love of other people.

But I can find fulfillment only in you. You do not ask about what I have achieved in life, about what I possess, or about the power that I have over others. You want to know only what I have made of myself.

Give me, then, an understanding of myself, honesty, patience, and humility. Then I shall be able to go forward, full of hope and trust, to meet my fulfillment in you.

What no eye has seen, nor ear heard, nor the heart of man conceived, what God has prepared for those who love him.

1 Corinthians 2:9

Lord, let me always remember that I am going toward a goal in life and that I shall eventually have to leave this world. Let me recognize what is of lasting value. Let me go on looking for what is of permanent importance in your eyes. Free me from everything that separates me from you.

Hermann Bezzel

Bless the Lord, O my soul;
and all that is within me,
bless his holy name!
Bless the Lord, O my soul,
and forget not all his benefits,
who forgives all your iniquity,
who heals all your diseases,
who redeems your life from the pit,
who crowns you with steadfast love and
mercy.
The Lord is merciful and gracious,
slow to anger and abounding in
steadfast love. . . .
He does not deal with us according to
our sins,
nor requite us according to our
iniquities. . . .
As a father pities his children,
so the Lord pities those who fear him.

Psalm 103:1- 4, 8, 10, 13

Time does not simply consist of hours and minutes. It also consists of love and affection. We have little time if we have little love.

Alexander Vinet

I Am of Good Will

God, you gave me my will so that I might choose and do good. How good it is that I am not led away from you by temptations and distractions, but that my love is constantly directed toward you and that all my strength can be used to do your will.

Prevent me, then, from giving way to temptations and from making mistakes. There is so much to disconcert me. Prevent me too from being negligent and forgetful. There is so much to distract me.

Give me great love, Lord, so that I can go on clinging to you and come closer and closer to you. Give me the strength to carry on in your service without tiring. Give me the courage not to let the inner flame of faith go out.

Give me a gentle disposition and a pure insight, so that I can look for you in everything.

Adalbert Stifter

Lord, help me be for everyone
the one who waits for the other without becoming impatient,
who listens without becoming tired,
who accepts with thanks and gives with love,
who is always available when he is needed,
the one to whom you can go when you are in need,
who radiates peace from within
and who belongs totally to you and is therefore open to others.

Foyer, Notre Dame Cathedral

We exhort you, brethren, admonish the idle, encourage the fainthearted, help the weak, be patient with them all.

See that none of you repays evil for evil, but always seek to do good to one another and to all. Rejoice always, pray

*constantly, give thanks in all
circumstances, for this is the will of
God in Christ Jesus for you.*

1 Thessalonians 5:14-18

Blessed are they who are understanding when my step is uncertain and my hand is trembling.

Blessed are they who realize that my ears can no longer hear everything.

Blessed are they who accept that I can no longer see so well and can no longer follow them so quickly.

Blessed are they who show no sign when I spill my food.

Blessed are they who stop for a moment to have a chat with me.

Blessed are they who never say: "You have already said that before."

Blessed are they who let me talk about the past.

Blessed are they who let me feel that they love me and that I am not alone.

Blessed are they who respect me and do not deprive me of my dignity.

Blessed are they who show me sympathy when I find it difficult to carry my cross.

Blessed are they who, in their goodness, help me find my way to God the Father and his goodness.

Ester May Walker

Steadfast and True

To be steadfast is a great virtue, a gift from you. You, Lord, want us to be steadfast in pursuit of the good. It is distasteful to you when we hesitate to choose the good and are wavering. But obstinacy is equally distasteful.

What we must give again and again is love. Quite simply and unquestioningly, we must be steadfast and true.

Again and again you show me your affection. Let me, then, hand on your goodness again and again to everyone who needs it. In this way I shall be steadfast in pursuing good and be open to your love.

No one can deny that you are faithful. This knowledge comforts us, even though we have to accuse ourselves of weakness with regard to temptation, slowness in doing good, and faithlessness toward you. It is comforting for us to know that, despite all our faithlessness, you are always faithful.

Sören Kierkegaard

We recoil from our own sins when we see them in others.

Goethe

Bearing with Others

Help me, Lord, to accept others as they are. Help me too to bear with others when their ideas differ from my own. So often we want everyone to share our opinions and think as we do. If I defend the truth, let me do it lovingly, so that no one is hurt.

I want to love the truth, but I must also love people. So I must first try to understand others. Then I will more easily be able to bear with them. You have, after all, made my fellow men over to me and want me to love them with all my heart.

Even if another person is quite different from me, let me remember this: you love all of us. Help me, then, not simply to bear with others, but to love them fully, with all my heart.

Forget it at once when someone has hurt you, but do not forget it if he has been kind.

Confucius

For me, it is no less virtuous to be able to remain silent than it is to be able to speak well. I think therefore that a man should have a neck as long as a crane's, so that, when he wants to speak, his words would have to go round very many bends before they reach his mouth.

Brother Giles

Love Peace

Let me, Lord, choose peace, not conflict.
Let me forgo being right, if good triumphs.
Let me recognize how limited my ideas are.
Let me accept all people as they are.
Let me be sensitive to what all people want.
Let me be aware of everyone's good will and good intention.

I will then ungrudgingly serve what is good and help to see that your will is done.

It is very strange, but when it comes to grumbling and quarreling, even the shyest among us has plenty to say. But when something friendly or placatory has to be said, then all we can do is wriggle, twist, and stammer.

Auerbach

Hallowed be thy name
— not mine;
thy kingdom come

— not mine;
thy will be done
— not mine.

Give us peace with you,
peace with other people,
peace with ourselves,
and deliver us from anxiety.

Dag Hammarskjold

Good Habits

I am in the habit of living and behaving
in a certain way. Even my thoughts
and ideas follow a certain pattern. The
experience that I have gained in all
the years of my life is very useful to
me now; it gives form to my life.

But do not let me become rigid,
Lord, in my habits. Help me to remain
open to all the new experience that
you hold in readiness for me.

Through the unforeseen events in
my life you are always preparing
surprises for me. Prevent me from
becoming enclosed in my own familiar
habits and from being deaf to your
voice.

Keep me open to you, Lord, and receptive. Give me the strength to adjust without difficulty to new situations. Give me the courage to make a new beginning — again and again. Sweep aside everything that prevents me from doing your will.

I am still on the way toward you. I still do not know how to believe and pray properly. But I am glad that my life has been so full and I thank you for this.

We should never give up hope. We should never cease to believe in the power of good will. We should never be downhearted or think that it is impossible to fight against fate. We should never lose our trust in what is good. Even now, so many splendid and courageous people bear witness to what is good, so long as we can discover them.

Paul VI

Through what I do I can share in God's creative power.

Teilhard de Chardin

Choose the best. If you are used to doing this, it will become easy and even pleasant.

Pythagoras

Respect

Lord, let me not lose my respect for people and things. Nowadays almost everything is systematically studied and there is a great deal of organization in our world. We all think that we have complete mastery over everything.

But we cannot understand everything. There is a great deal that is beyond our powers of penetration. Ultimately, however, you are always there, Lord. Your love gives value and meaning to everything.

Let me, Lord, continue to respect people and things. In this, I shall encounter you.

Everyone who has respect is a believer. Everyone who is dependent and responsible in the whole of his being and accepts this, both inwardly and outwardly, is a believer.

Otto Karrer

We treat others with the respect that we have for ourselves.

Joseph Kuhnel

Lost property — nothing lost
Lost heart — a great deal lost
Lost honor — even more lost
Lost soul — everything lost.

Keeping a Secret

Help me, Lord, to keep any secret that has been entrusted to me. There are too many people who are only too anxious to find out secrets and things that should remain concealed and to talk about them without love.

Help me to be silent, Lord, even though I may find it difficult. Let me keep any secret entrusted to me as if it were a precious gift.

Leave my heart free, so that anyone can confide in me. You, after all, are the one who sends people to me. It is because of you that I am able to show love to my fellow men.

That is why I will try to keep any secret entrusted to me, for your sake.

It is absurd how people who blurt out secrets almost always ask those to whom they tell those secrets not to repeat them. In this way, they admit that they are themselves wrong.

Anyone who asks others to keep a secret ought to remain silent himself. Then he would have been able to keep the original secret. But since he has already disclosed it, there is no reason to ask others to keep it.

St. John Chrysostom

Good speech is made better by good silence.

Rumor increases by being spread.

Happy and Cheerful

Lord, keep me happy and cheerful. Preserve my sense of humor. Let me always be ready to take part in good, positive conversation.

If my life is darkened by suffering, do not let me complain. Do not let me be sad or despairing.

Do not let me be elated and do not let me be selfish in a superficial search for pleasure.

Let me be sensitive and tactful in my contacts with others and help them find something beautiful in every experience.

You are my God. This makes me happy. Let my happiness be seen by others.

Rejoice in the Lord always; again I say, Rejoice. Let all men know your forbearance. The Lord is at hand. Have no anxiety about anything, but in everything by prayer and supplication with thanksgiving let your requests be made known to God. And the peace of God, which passes all understanding, will keep your hearts and your minds in Christ Jesus.

Philippians 4:4-7

Lord, let every one of us be completely convinced that everything comes from you. Then neither joy nor sorrow will be able to separate us from you. Help us to look for you and stay close to you both in joy and in sorrow.

One man likes improving his property, another breeding better horses. I take pleasure in making sure that I become a better person every day.

Socrates

I do not ask, Lord, for worldly pleasures. These will not make me better. I ask for your Spirit.

Send me your Spirit, Lord, to illuminate me. Strengthen my trust in you. Let me persevere in this to the end.

The man who is always happy must be a good man. He may not be the cleverest, but he can always achieve what the cleverest man wants to achieve with all his cleverness.

Friedrich Nietzsche

Lord, we pray especially for all cheerful people. Their happiness is infectious. Let them remain cheerful and show them the way to yourself and to eternal happiness.

The way that you choose to make another person happy does not matter — just make him happy.

Ovid

Lord, thank you for letting me live. Even though I may have many cares — including all the little everyday worries — and am aware that there are many difficulties still in store for me, I am still glad that I am alive and that there is something for me to do.

I thank you too, Lord, that I can still enjoy all that you go on giving me in

your love: the beauty of nature, the
goodness of my fellow men, the joy of
my own heart, and the knowledge that
you love, accept, and bless me.

Lord, give me a good digestion
and something to digest.
   Give me a healthy body
and the ability
to keep it as healthy as possible.
   Give me a holy soul, Lord,
so that I shall always know what is
good and pure
and not be afraid
when I see sin,
but look for a way
of putting everything in order.
   Give me a holy soul, Lord,
so that I shall not know
what it is to be bored
and shall not complain,
sigh, or grumble.
   Do not let me, Lord,
worry too much
about what takes up so much space
in my life —
what I call "me."

Lord, give me a sense of humor.
Give me the grace
to understand a joke,
so that I can have a little happiness
and share it with others.

St. Thomas More

One day's sorrow lasts longer than a month's joy.

A happy face spreads light everywhere.

The Beauty of Life

You have given me a great deal of happiness, Lord, and I am grateful to you because I can enjoy it.

All my life, I have tried to achieve something and to become someone. Even now, when my strength is failing me, life still has much to offer. I thank you, Lord, for all the beauty that is present in my life.

I also pray for the future. Keep my mind and spirit open so that I can go on discovering the beauty of life. Let the end of my life also be beautiful, since I shall then go to you, the fullness of beauty and my happiness.

Let me go on happily and peacefully enjoying my old age. I may miss the pleasure that I took in being active when I was younger, but I am still very grateful to you, because my greatest pleasure is to live in the knowledge that you love me and that you have so abundantly blessed my life.

I want to believe in the angel that lives in man.

Carl Sonnenschein

Lord, be in front of us to lead us;
be behind us to urge us on;
be beneath us to support us;
be above us to bless us;
be around us to protect us;
be in us to fill us.

Let our spirit, soul, and body
serve you well
and glorify your name.

Nathan Soderblom

If you see your life as a task, it is not difficult to go on living.

Marie von Ebner-Eschenbach

What comes from God does not have to be embellished by men. It is even averse to human embellishment. It comes straight up to us as we are and raises us up.

Queen Wilhelmina

Fulfillment with You

So much is done for us today. We are very grateful for this, but there is a danger that it will make us lose sight of the future.

We will not cease to think of the end of our life that we are approaching, the fulfillment of our being with you in eternity.

So little is said about the end of our life. Help us, Lord, so that the last stage in our journey will really be fulfillment. May we always have people around us who believe in you and will help us to complete our journey through life as Christians.

The present is the only time that we can really control. We must use it as God wants us to.

Blaise Pascal

Patience

Lord, make me patient. Let me endure weakness and evil. Let me be patient with myself. Let me not despair if I am not as I would like to be or as others would like me to be or as I think I ought to be for you. It is not easy to spend one's life combating one's own weakness and, again and again, have to make a new beginning. But if you are patient with me, then I will be patient too.

Let me be patient with my fellow men. It is often difficult to put up with them. So often they seem to think so highly of themselves, simply because they are fitter and younger than I am. They even try to boss me around as though they had a monopoly of truth and power.

But we are all weak and we all have faults. You are right to expect us to carry each other's burdens. If you are patient with everyone, then I will be patient too.

Lord, make me patient. Let me endure weakness and evil. I need patience. Be patient with me.

Good sense makes a man slow to anger,
and it is his glory to overlook an offense.

Proverbs 19:11

Take my yoke upon you and learn from me; for I am gentle and lowly of heart and you will find rest for your souls.

Matthew 11:29

Lead a life worthy of the calling to which you have been called, with all lowliness and meekness, with patience, forbearing one another in love.

Ephesians 4:1-2

You, Lord, are our creator and you must find it difficult to endure pride in your creatures and, in spite of everything, go on loving us.

Thank you for being so patient. So long as you are patient, there is hope for me.

The person who is always impatient is living in the future.
He imagines that future today — as it will never be.

Gustav Radbruch

Everything here on earth is changeable, Lord, and I shall never find peace. Let me look for peace with you. You have prepared for us a glory that is beyond our power of imagination.

If you have not achieved what you wanted to achieve in the spiritual life, this is certainly not because you have not fasted every day. If, however, you had tried to be patient with yourself, you would have made up for a great deal. And if you had been patient both with yourself and with your neighbor, God would have given you a great deal of grace.

Daniel Considine

Patience makes everything light.

Patience is greater than learning.

Impatience is self-torment.

Goodness

Give me goodness and love, Lord, so that I can love others from the fullness of my own heart. Let me do as you do: love others as you love us, whom you gave your life for. You have poured love into our hearts so that we can give it to others. Help me, then, make others happy by handing on goodness and love.

A good word is worth more than a gift.

Sirach 18:16

It often happens that you become good only when you are old. It is then that you begin to feel really sorry for failing so frequently in goodness.

Maria von Ebner-Eschenbach

Do not be overcome by evil, but overcome evil with good.

Romans 12:21

Lord, help me to distinguish more and more clearly between my will and yours. Let me keep a much more careful watch on myself and become much more open to you. Help me to be less concerned with my own interests and to give much more time serving you and others who need my help.

If you are in good spirits
you will do good things.

Repentance is the month of May among the virtues.

Contentment

Let me be contented in the knowledge that you are near me. Let me also be contented with myself, because you want me to be as I am. Let me not be jealous of others, looking at them and comparing them with myself, thinking about their possessions, their appearance, their influence and their power.

I should long only for you. I should be happy with what you give me. You have surely given me quite enough. Let me, then, be satisfied with it. Let me be quite contented with your gifts.

It is only through you, God, that the things of this world become valuable. But we can also recognize their value if we are contented and use and enjoy them thankfully.

Let me be contented and let me always thank you for your love.

A good man is a contented man.

Never forget that you need very little to live a happy life.

Marcus Aurelius

If we have food and clothing, with these we shall be content. But those who desire to be rich fall into temptation, into a snare, into many senseless and hurtful desires that plunge men into ruin and destruction.

1 Timothy 6:8-9

I must serve God in a special way. That is why he has created me. He has entrusted me alone with a special task, and no other. I have my own work, my own mission. . . .
  In some way I am necessary to him for the carrying out of his plans. . . . Of course, he can put another person in my place if I let the matter rest — just as he can beget sons of Abraham from stones. Yet I still have my own share in that great work. . . .

God created me for a purpose. I have to do something good and carry out his work. I can be an angel of peace or proclaim the truth — without directly aiming to — simply by keeping his commandments and serving him in my work.

Cardinal Newman

The Things of This World

We are proud of the things that we have done, Lord, but every one of our achievements is a gift from you. Prevent us, then, from seeing the things around us as aims in themselves. We do not want to boast about what we have achieved. Nor do we want to envy others for having done more than we have. We want to be neither self-satisfied nor dissatisfied with ourselves.

Protect us from prejudice, which may prevent us from being aware of true values, and let us not attach too much importance to the things of this world. Poverty can stifle man's desire for salvation, but riches can lead to a blunting of our spirit.

Let us use the things of this world thankfully. You have given them to us and they are a way to eternal fulfillment.

There is a suffocating form of poverty in the world today that can be expressed in the words "I have no one." There is no one with time for me, no one to help me, listen to me, comfort me or care for me.

As long as I was working, I did not notice it so much, but now that I am old, I find it suffocating.

Our greatest enemy is not a painful void, it is suffering from a surfeit. Our hearts are no longer restless. Our religious practices and our prayer have become routine. The spirit has gone from them. We speak impressively with our lips, but not from our hearts. We hit out angrily as soon as we are frustrated. All this is dangerous to the life of the spirit.

Friedrich Dessauer

Woe to you that are rich, for you have received your consolation. Woe to you that are full, for you shall hunger. Woe to you that laugh, for you shall mourn and weep. Woe to you when all men speak well of you, for so their fathers did to the false prophets.

Luke 6:24-26

An Instrument of Love

Make me an instrument of love and peace.

Let me bring love where there is hatred, forgiveness where there is guilt, unity where there is discord, truth where there is error, light where there is darkness, happiness where there is sorrow.

I am here not to be satisfied, but to console, not to be understood, but to understand, not to be loved, but to love.

Because, if we give, we receive, if we forgive, we are forgiven, if we die, we enter new life.

St. Francis of Assisi

A Channel of Your Peace

Lord, make me a channel of your peace.

Where there is hatred, let me bring love. Where there is offense, forgiveness. Where there is discord, reconciliation. Where there is doubt, faith. Where there is despair, hope. Where there is sadness, joy. Where there is darkness, your light. If we give, we are made rich. If we forget ourselves, we find peace. If we forgive, we receive forgiveness. If we die, we receive eternal resurrection.

Give us peace, Lord.

St. Francis of Assisi

I would say this to everyone who is employed in any way in the care of old people and to all old people themselves. Your life and work can be an expression of deep, warm humanity and of the true spirit of the Gospel, which is Good News for all men, a message that is also given by

people to others through their mutual
love and care.

Cardinal Alfrink

Begin by thinking "yes."
Be good, according to the other
person's needs.
Value each other.
Take the other person as he is, not as
you would like him to be.
Help your fellow man in his humanity.
Forgive each other.
Live what you learn.
Do not command or forbid when it is
not strictly necessary.
Present God sympathetically to other
people.
Remember that there is a place for
humor.

The Ten Commandments of Love
of One's Neighbor

Love can manage all things; love can
see the best in everything; love makes
what is bitter sweet; love is the

foundation of all enjoyment; love leads to great comfort.

Jacob Cats

We know from experience that love does not consist of looking at each other, but of looking together in the same direction.

Antoine de Saint-Exupéry

It is not what man does that makes him meaningful. His life is meaningful if he acts morally as a Christian.

Being a Christian is also being available with all the strength at one's disposal for others, building up a life with others and bearing each other's burdens.

This is not productive in the ordinary sense of the word. It is productive, however, in that it enriches man's existence.

Paschasius of Marvilde

IV. Going On Living

A Beautiful Old Age

Lord, I thank you that I am living at a time when we can be assured of care in our old age. I have worked for many years. I have given time and strength. Now I can be looked after.

Keep me fit and cheerful. Let me enjoy a peaceful old age. Let me go on being active spiritually and let me be more and more conscious of the inner values of life. What use would it be for me to have health, and time to enjoy it, if my life were meaningless?

That is why I ask you to give me true joy.

People have no idea of how useful uselessness can be.

Martin Buber

Those very active people who think that they have seen, heard, and done everything better than others — for all their intense activity, they have seen only the outside of life.

If we regularly stand still, turn inward, and look, we shall gain insight into the depths of things.

Johannes Adam

Lord, help me to turn inward. Deep within me, quite hidden, is the power to come into contact with you. Touch me inwardly and make me ready for my future life in you.

Be happy with your life; it is later than you think.

Do Not Leave Me

Do not leave me, Lord, now that I am old. If you do, life will cease to be attractive. Life is not easy. It changes so quickly all the time.

There are so many difficult technical problems and the solutions seem to be to build more and more apparatuses.

So many different people and civilizations come into our lives on the television screen, but there is no one to take our personal difficulties or sorrows seriously, or simply ask us how we are getting on.

Our lives have been made longer by medical science, and there are many drugs to choose from, but we still have to endure the troubles of old age and wait for someone to help us.

And if we can no longer manage at home, we have to go to live in an old people's home. We have to learn how to get on with others in a community where we do not always feel quite at home. There is often nothing much for us to do and we become bored because we rely on the help of other people.

And outside, life continues at high speed. There is so much traffic and it seems to take no notice of us. There is no longer any pleasure to be had in going out. We have to be satisfied with watching events on the TV and reading about what is happening.

Progress continues, more and more

quickly. It has overtaken us and we have remained behind.

So do not leave me, Lord, now that I am old. If you do, life will cease to be attractive.

Be like men who are waiting for their master to come home from the marriage feast, so that they may open to him at once when he comes and knocks. Blessed are those servants whom the master finds awake when he comes. Truly, he will gird himself and have them sit at table and he will come and serve them.

Luke 12:36-37

Lord, do not conceal yourself from me
when I conceal myself from you.
You know I am afraid of you,
that I avoid you, yet still long for you.
Do not go past my heart.

Do not be angry with me
when I fail to show you love.
I name you, but I do not know you.
I bend down before you, but not inwardly,
and when I pray it is reluctantly.

You must speak the right word in me,
Lord.
Everytime I find words for you,
I hide away, disguised, from you.
But now, O Lord, I wait for you to come
and speak to me, while I, your servant,
listen.

Lord, call me like a lost sheep
that has not looked for and cannot find
you.
Let me, as one whom you love
and as your own child,
hear your voice in my sleep.

Muus Jacobse

Old Age Is Meaningful

I think that old age is meaningful. Even
though work is much less important
and I have much less strength, my life
is still evolving. This growth continues
from the moment I was born until the
end. And behind it all are you and I,
your creature. You created me to live
and be happy. Your love keeps me
going.

I believe that my life is meaningful, because you wanted me and because you still love me and bless me. That is why I am confident that you will make me happy in eternity.

It is not so bad to lose your life, but it is unbearable to think that your life will lose its meaning.

Albert Camus

When you are officially pensioned off, you naturally think: Now I am really old. I am an old-age pensioner.

We have a right to our pensions. But we also have to realize that we have ceased to work and no longer have the function we used to have.

We have to realize that there is *a time to keep and a time to cast away.* If we know this, we shall be mature.

But life goes on, and we have other rights and duties.

If the only meaning of life were what we could grasp with our very limited human understanding, life would not be worth living.

Oswald Bumke

At first sight, it would seem that we have to thank doctors for making it possible for us to live about fifteen years longer than people did not so very long ago. In fact, there is another, deeper reason: God wants to give us respite after all those hectic years and let us find time for him.

God wants to open our eyes to the reality of the supernatural during the quiet years of our old age, when we have the approach of death in view. If we look at our life and give it form and meaning in the light of eternity, we shall learn the art of growing old.

The most important thing is *not* to retain our faculties as long as possible or to improve them. God can make good use of us even without our faculties. For him, there is no useless old person.

Feeling good or doing something impressive — this is not what gives meaning to our lives. The only thing that really matters is to give ourselves entirely to God, with all our heart, all our soul, and all our strength, and not remain attached in any way at all to the past.

This clinging to God is what gives meaning to our old age.

Theodore Bovet

Lord, send me what you want —
happiness or sorrow.
It is enough for me to know
that both come from you.
But do not overwhelm me
with joy or suffering;
I am not strong enough to contain
them.

Eduard Mörike

Work and Success

When I was young, I used to love to "get down" to work. I was enthusiastic. I liked to exert myself. I was very pleased with myself whenever I was able to do something. And I took it all for granted.

It was only when I became older that I began to realize that you gave me all those things: health and strength and the ability to work.

I want to thank you now for every day of my life and for all the work you still let me do.

Man is worth only what he is worth to God — no more and no less. The value of old age cannot be measured in what we do, but in what we are. It is a fulfillment: carrying to the end the task that we are set by life.

When we reach the end of this life, however, life does not simply break off, it enters fulfillment. There is no ultimate fulfillment here on earth. In old age, we have the task of preparing ourselves for our encounter with God.

Lord, give me clear eyes
to see the world's need.
Give me sharp ears
to hear your call.
Give me gentle hands
for the suffering of all men.
Give me clear words of hope

for this confused time.
Give me good feet
to go to work for others,
and a soul, quiet and modest,
in which your peace is found.

Life is often difficult for people. Work
exhausts them, and it is not always
made easier by machines. Machines
require constant attention and this
often has a very bad effect on the
nerves. Repeated demands are made
on people and more and more is
asked of them, yet hardly any thought
is given to the very people who are
expected to do so much.

Help all those who work for us, Lord.
Do not let them become inwardly
impoverished. Do not let them lose
their strength. Give them moments
when they can come to themselves
again. Despite the pressures of their
work, let them remain good and not
lose touch with the people around
them. Give them patience with us old
people and let them love us a little.
Help them find their way to you.

Sometimes a great deal is done. But then nothing is really ever done, because what ought to be done is not done.

Myller

God, all good comes from you. Let us see what is good and with your help do it. Whenever we are in need, let us trust in your goodness and be confident that you will protect us. Turn away all that may harm us and help us to be good.

He told them a parable, saying, "The land of a rich man brought forth plentifully and he thought to himself, 'What shall I do, for I have nowhere to store my crops?' And he said, 'I will do this: I will pull down my barns and build larger ones; and there I will store all my grain and my goods. And I will say to my soul, Soul, you have ample goods laid up for many years; take your ease, eat, drink and be merry.' But God said to him, 'Fool! This night your soul is required of you; and the things you

*have prepared, whose will they be?' So
is he who lays up treasure for himself
and is not rich toward God."*

Luke 12:16-21

For Those Who Are Hard of Hearing

My hearing has become less good. I
cannot hear as well as I did when I
was younger. A great deal of what is
going on does not penetrate.

In the past it was quite different. I
could hear everything. I could hear
people talking and singing, praying
and being happy. A great deal
penetrated even deeper — to my
heart. Your words, Lord, gave me
strength and courage. They comforted
me and gave me confidence.

Now everything has changed. Most
things I can only hear with difficulty
and some things escape me
completely. And people do not like
talking to someone if they have to
shout to make themselves understood. That is why I cannot talk in
confidence with anyone very often

now. I often feel unhappy about this.
Help me, Lord, to bear this cross.

*Truly, truly, I say to you, he who hears
my word and believes him who sent me
has eternal life. He does not come into
judgment, but has passed from death to
life.*

John 5:24

Lord,
I do not listen to your word
because someone told me
that you were God's son.
   I listen to it
because it is more beautiful
than any word that man has ever
spoken.
   In your word,
I recognize that you are God's son.

André Gide

It is not enough just to tell people the
truth. You have to be very insistent in
making them conscious of it.

Unfortunately, their first reaction is to turn away from it.

Georges Bernanos

Blessed are those who hear the word of God and keep it!

Luke 11:28

Has the world ever been changed by anything other than ideas and their magic vehicle — words?

Thomas Mann

Your word has remained with me, Lord. I have come to know it well from Holy Scripture, hymns, and prayer. Now that I can no longer easily hear the words that other people speak, I can still go on talking and listening to you. Despite my troubles, I can be glad that your word is always near to me in Jesus Christ. That is a comfort to me.

Let me listen carefully to every word you say to me. Let me take it to heart and let me keep it in patience, so that it bears fruit.

*Let me hear what God the Lord will
speak,*
for he will speak peace to his people,
*to his saints, to those who turn to him in
their hearts.*
  *Surely salvation is at hand for those
who fear him,*
that glory may dwell in our land.

Psalm 85:8-9

For Those Who Cannot See Well

I can no longer see as well as I did
when I was younger. My sight is less
clear. A great deal of what is
happening around me escapes me.

Previously, however, I also was
unable to see everything well. I was
often deceived by appearances in the
world. I frequently thought that things
that were really valueless were
genuine.

Although you have always been with
me, I did not always see you, Lord, as
you really are. Now my eyes are
weaker, but I can see more clearly. I
can see you much more clearly.

Your word is light for my soul. Behind everything that happens, let me see you more and more clearly.

For me, it is often a blessing not to be able to see something.

August Strindberg

Even as it becomes darker around me, there is still a great deal to make me happy. Even the memory of things past can be beautiful. I thank you for having made everything so good and so beautiful.

Let me go on seeing clearly inwardly. Let me never lose sight of you. Let this continue until I am able to contemplate you in perfect light.

What no eye has seen, nor ear heard, nor the heart of man conceived,
What God has prepared for those who love him,
God has revealed to us through the Spirit.

*For the Spirit searches everything, even
the depths of God.*

1 Corinthians 2:9-10

**Everything in the world is there only
for the one who has eyes to see it.**

Eduard Spranger

**If we shut our eyes,
the world is at an end.**

What the Cross Can Tell Us

*For the word of the cross is folly to
those who are perishing, but to us who
are being saved it is the power of God.
For it is written, "I will destroy the
wisdom of the wise, and the cleverness
of the clever I will thwart. . . . ."*

*Where is the wise man through the
folly of what we preach to save those
who believe?*

*The Jews demand signs and the
Greeks seek wisdom, but we preach
Christ crucified, a stumbling block to
Jews and folly to Gentiles, but to those*

*who are called, both Jews and Greeks,
the power of God and the wisdom of
God. For the foolishness of God is
wiser than men and the weakness of
God is stronger than men.*

1 Corinthians 1:18-19, 21:25

The cross has not been taken from my
shoulders and I have often asked why
not. Why am I still so frequently put to
the test? The answer can be found
with You.

Of all the means at your disposal
that, as a man, you might have chosen
to redeem human nature, you chose to
suffer. You redeemed us by suffering
and dying on the cross.

Philosophers have always sought
salvation in knowledge. Politicians
have used power to solve all
problems. Rich people have looked to
amusement and pharisees have
sought selfjustification. But you took
up your cross and gave your life for us.

You are right to expect us to love
you more in suffering and being put to
the test. Help us, then, in all that we
have to endure, to encounter you in it.

Among the invalids lying in the porticos beside the pool of Bethesda was a man who had been ill for thirty-eight years. When Jesus saw him and knew that he had been lying there a long time, he said to him, "Do you want to be healed?" The sick man answered him, "Sir, I have no man to put me into the pool". .... Jesus said to him, "Rise, take up your pallet and walk." And at once the man was healed.

John 5:5-9

Dear friends, think of this:
every house has its cross.
If it isn't outside, then it's inside.
If it isn't God's cross,
then it isn't God's house.

Adriaan Poirters

Bless Me in My Sickness

Lord Jesus Christ, help me. Protect me and keep my spirits up. Bless me.

Lord, bend over me. Forgive me my sins. Cure me and save my soul. Let me long more and more for what is good. Give me your peace.

God the Father, you have created me. God the Son, you died for me on the cross. God the Holy Spirit, you were given to me when I was baptized. Make me well.

God, show me your favor and save my body and soul. Preserve me from all evil and let me do only good.

Lord, bless me and protect me. Let your face shine over me. Turn toward me and give me peace.

I consider that the sufferings of this present time are not worth comparing with the glory that is to be revealed to us. . . . We know that the whole creation has been groaning in travail together until now; and not only creation, but we ourselves, who have the first fruits of the Spirit, groan inwardly as we wait for adoption as sons, the redemption of our bodies. For in this hope we were saved.

Romans 8:18, 22-24

The Infirmities of Old Age

I want to accept the infirmities of old age patiently from you. I want to do something to make up for my sins and to be a blessing for those who are dear to me. I do not want to complain or be dissatisfied.

I know that you are good to me and that you are to be found hidden behind everything. I thank you for giving me something and for taking something away from me.

All that I ask is that I should not lose sight of you in the sufferings of every day.

In the whole of the world there is really only one problem, one single problem: how to show people the spiritual meaning of their existence, how to give them a kind of spiritual longing, a holy restlessness. . . . In the long run, you cannot live on refrigerators, politics, speculations on the stock exchange, and crossword puzzles. It just doesn't work.

Antoine de Saint-Exupéry

By allowing us to suffer you show us that you want to draw us closer to you. Let us always find you in joy and sorrow.

It is not what we do that counts, but why and how we do it. More important than what we say is what we do, and more important than what we do are our reasons for doing it.

Louis Evely

Lord, you know that I am getting older and that I shall soon be really old.

Help me, Lord, not to become a garrulous old person who has to express a strong opinion about everything and cannot stop talking.

Prevent me from thinking that I can and must go on arranging other people's affairs and from imagining that it would be terrible if they did not benefit from my great wisdom and experience.

But *do* let me have a few friends who are similar to myself, because I know I shall need them.

I hardly dare to ask you to give me the strength to be able to listen to other people's complaints about their troubles and sufferings all the time with great sympathy. All I ask is that you will help me put up with annoying people with the necessary patience.

I ask you, too, to prevent me from talking all the time about my own little troubles and sufferings. I know that they will increase as the years go by and that the inclinations to be preoccupied with them will become more difficult for me to resist.

I hardly dare ask you to keep me healthy in mind and spirit; it would be better for me if you sent me a little humility and made me less obstinate and less inclined to think that I am always right. I should like to have a little more insight into myself and to recognize that I can sometimes make mistakes.

Help me to judge others kindly. I don't think I shall ever be a saint — people who think they are saints are often unbearable — but do not let me become a shrewish old woman who is always prompt to point out what is wrong.

I would rather that you made me someone who can live in sympathy with others without being sentimental and who is always ready to help them without forcing herself on them.

Teach me how to discover goodness and fine aspects in people whom I have not expected to be good, in whom I have not looked for such things. And let me, Lord, be friendly enough to let them know that I have made these discoveries.   Amen.

Margot Benary-Isbert

Wisdom Comes from Suffering

You are certainly not indifferent, Lord, to what happens to us. You always hold us in your hand, even when we are ill and have to suffer.

You do not mete suffering out to us. You do not want to torment us. Suffering must be a means — a way that will lead us to you.

You do not want us to have to suffer,

but you are pleased when we accept our suffering in the right way and thereby come closer to you.

Help me discover your presence in everything and never doubt that you love me.

The kingdom of God begins with the cross.

Cardinal Alfred Bengsch

If someone does not want to bear his cross, he has to bear with himself. The question is, which is the more difficult to do?

Emanuel von Bodman

Blessed be the God and Father of our Lord Jesus Christ, the Father of mercies and God of all comfort, who comforts us in all our affliction, so that we may be able to comfort those who are in any affliction with the comfort with which we ourselves are comforted by God. For as we share abundantly in

*Christ's sufferings, so through Christ
we share abundantly in comfort too.*

2 Corinthians 1:3-5

Lord, let me not be blind and
indifferent to the sufferings of my
fellow men. Open my eyes so that I
can also see their hidden needs. Open
my heart so that I will help them gladly
and quickly.

There has been a good deal of
discussion recently about various
theologies — a theology of action, a
theology of revolution, and so on.
More than about a theology of the
cross. These theologies often lack an
understanding of the value of
suffering. Because of this, they cannot
tell us much about the value of those
who are visited by suffering.

Yet the cross is a reality in our
world. At least a third of the world's
population is bowed down under the
weight of it.

Jesus blessed us much more
through his suffering and death than

through his preaching and activity. His suffering and death brought the resurrection. And surely that also applies to other people!

We must therefore choose the cross through which Christ redeemed us. We must have a positive attitude toward illness and suffering, in the knowledge that our salvation is to be found there.

Anton Gots

Compared with the wisdom of your suffering,
our drudgery seems very foolish.
Suffering is meaningful —
it can lead us to you.
We cannot be saved by riches and power.
Only the love that you give us
can save us.
With your love we can bear anything.
Even though I am put severly to the test,
I know that you love me.
Give me the strength
to bear everything in such a way

that it is a positive response to your
love.
   I want to suffer now,
until you take my suffering from me
and give me happiness forever.
I thank you with all my heart.

*The crucible is for silver
and the furnace is for gold,
but the Lord tries hearts.*

Proverbs 17:3

I do not ask you for health or sickness.
I do not ask you for life or death. What
I ask is that you will dispose life and
death, in my case of health and
sickness, to your glory and my
salvation, for the benefit of the Church
and for the sake of your saints. Only
you know what is good for me.

Blaise Pascal

Your Will

I take the good things in my life for
granted, as though I had a right to
them.

Trying to know your will and do it —
this I do not take so much for granted,
especially when I find it difficult.

Help me, Lord, not to be dissatisfied
and frustrated when I am prevented
from doing my own will and when
things don't go as I want them to go.

Give me the strength, when I am
tested by suffering, to do what you
want me to do with my life.

I am conscious of your presence
with me as I go through life. Let me
think of this when life is difficult.

*Blessed is the man who endures trial,
for when he has stood the test he will
receive the crown of life which God has
promised to those who love him.*

James 1:12

Every morning you can make an
entirely new beginning. You can let
what made you angry and what
frustrated you yesterday slip away
from you, and indeed you must do this.
What is more, you must not begin
again to plan and make calculations,
trying to get the better of people.

Look at your fellow men every morning as though they were quite new to you and be ready to love and admire them from the depths of your heart.

Gilbert Cesbron

There are remedies that you can use for illness, but there are none that you can use to protect yourself against God's will.

Make Me Happy

You give us joy and want us to be happy because you are happy yourself.

Make me cheerful. Drive all sadness from my soul. Help me overcome low spirits. Take all anxiety away from me.

Give me more and more happiness. Then I shall experience joy in everything I encounter.

Let your goodness and your grace be the source of real joy for me and let them give me the strength I need to bear with everything.

Make me happy, so that, from the rullness of my heart, I can make others happy and so bring light and sunshine into their lives.

You are never too old to be happy.

Wilhelm Kreiten

God loves a cheerful spirit. The smallest service offered to God or our neighbor with a smile on our face is worth more than all the suffering that we take on ourselves with a sour face.

Joseph Schorderer

Happy are the people whose God is the Lord!

Psalm 144:15

I would like to be happy enough to be able to make others happy.

Christian Morgenstern

To be happy that God exists and that we are his children — that is true joy.

Ferdinand Ebner

Lord, put an end to my longing to be happy and contented. Let me simply be glad in the certainty of your love. You give me food and clothing. You surround me with kind friends. You give me a home and you have made my old age secure.

But even if the outside circumstances of my life were to become less good or even really bad, I would still be able to stay inwardly peaceful and calm, because I do not look for happiness in things or even in people, but in you. Only you can make me permanently happy.

It is only when I possess you that the people and things around me are really valuable. It is only in you that I can find happiness everywhere and always. That is why I ask you to put an end to my longing to be happy and contented. Make me happy and contented simply in your love.

Even if my earthly possessions were very great, they would not compare with the strength and joy of a living faith.

Madeleine Sémer

Respect for God's Creatures

Thank you, Lord, for all birds and other creatures. They give me joy and a little insight into the mystery of life. We are, after all, your creatures and all of us share in the richness of life.

You have made the birds, fishes, and animals to be useful to man and to give him pleasure. You are therefore right to expect us, in return, to respect them.

I thank you for letting me experience your creation and ask you to let me see you, my loving Father, in all things.

You cannot imagine how dreary the world would be if there were no animals.

Elias Canetti

I cannot look into an animal's eyes
without feeling that I owe it something.

Isolde Kurz

We can see ourselves and our good
and bad qualities when we look at
animals.

Ernst Jünger

One day, when he was in Rimini, St.
Anthony went to the mouth of the river
near the sea and began to call the
fishes in God's name, as for a sermon,
saying:
"My fish brothers, you should give
as many thanks as you can to your
Creator, who has granted you such a
noble element as your dwelling place,
so that you have fresh and salt water,
just as you please. Moreover, he has
given you many refuges to escape
from storms. He has also given you a
clear and transparent element and
ways to travel and food to live on.
"When he created you, he gave you
the command to increase and multiply

and he gave you his blessing. Later, during the Flood, when all the other animals were perishing, God preserved you alone without loss. He has also given you fins so that you can swim wherever you wish. It was granted you, by the order of God, to keep alive Jonah, the prophet of God, and to cast him on to dry land safe and sound on the third day. You offered tribute money to our Lord Jesus Christ when, as a poor man, he had nothing to pay the tax. You were chosen as food for the eternal King, our Lord Jesus Christ, before his resurrection and in a mysterious way afterward.

"Because of all these things, you should praise and bless the Lord, who has given you so many more blessings than other creatures."

"Little Flowers" of St. Francis

Most high, all powerful, all good Lord!
All praise is yours, all glory, all honor
  and all blessing.
To you alone, Most High, do they belong.

No mortal lips are worthy
to pronounce your name.

All praise be yours, my Lord, through
all that you have made,
and first my lord Brother Sun,
who brings the day and light you
give us through him.
How beautiful he is, how radiant in all
his splendor!
Of you, Most High, he bears the
likeness.

All praise be yours, my Lord, through
Sisters Moon and Stars;
in the heavens you have made
them,
bright, precious, fair.

All praise be yours, my Lord, through
Brothers Wind and Air,
and, fair and stormy, through all the
weather's moods,
by which you cherish all that you
have made.

All praise be yours, my Lord, through
Sister Water,
  so useful and lowly,
  precious and pure.

All praise be yours, my Lord, through
Brother Fire,
  through whom you brighten up the
night.
How beautiful he is, how gay!
Full of power and strength.
All praise be yours, my Lord, through
Sister Earth,
  our mother who feeds us in her
sovereignty
  and produces fruits with colored
flowers and herbs.

All praise be yours, my Lord, through
those
  who grant pardon for love of you
  and through those who endure
sickness and trial.

Happy are those who endure in peace.
By you, Most High,
  they will be crowned.

All praise be yours, my Lord, through
Sister Death,
  from whose embrace
  no mortal can escape.

Woe to those who die in mortal sin!
Happy are those she finds doing your
will!
The second death can do no harm to
them.

Praise and bless my Lord
  and give him thanks
  and serve him with great humility.

> St. Francis: "The Canticle of
> Brother Sun"

Lonely and Alone

No one is alone.
  All of us have people around us
for whom we have to do something.
  What really matters
is what we do to each other.
  Let me always remember, Lord, that
it is up to me

to make people feel at home with me
— to feel secure and happy.

Man often needs the first half of his
life to discover that he is not alone and
the second half to make this discovery
a practical reality in his life.

Sigmund Graff

You have, in your goodness, given me
an abundance of love, happiness, and
peace. Help me to share those gifts
with others.

Are people becoming more lonely?
There are more and more people. The
cities are full of them. They always
crowd together. Life is getting longer
and, at the same time, duller and less
personal. There is less sense of
community in the family, among
friends, and in society generally.
Everyone is trying to manage his life
on his own.

Children feel neglected, young
people are disillusioned and full of

disordered passions, workers in enormous factories and offices feel wretched and unappreciated, and many marriages end badly. We live in difficult times.

People yearn more and more for human contacts, for warmth, security, and community, not in the great organizations of modern society but in small circles, at work, in the district where they live, in their family.

Who is my neighbor? The call for good fellow men becomes every day louder and more insistent.

Robert Svoboda

Lord, please help all those who are in conflict with others, and cannot find a way out, toward a solution to their problems.

I am always attentive to people and to whether they can manage to live with others. If they can, they are really carrying out the task of man and society.

Antoine de Saint-Exupéry

Do not leave me in the lurch now, Lord, as my body is becoming weaker and my strength is failing, at a time when wisdom and experience seem no longer appreciated, when everything that I have built and worked for is slowly but surely being taken from my hands and done by younger people. . . .

Do not let me feel lonely and deserted. You must go on being the meaning of my life.

Do not let me continue to insist on my rights when they have become empty and meaningless. Do not let me waste my time in such pursuits. Let me, rather, try to love others and find people who are ready to help me.

The forgetfulness that comes with old age offers us a good opportunity to get rid of a lot of rubbish — expectations that have not been fulfilled and mistakes that we have made. Also, very many superficial acquaintances disappear from sight and the space around me shrinks, until it is exactly the right size in which I can be really human.

Wilhelm von Scholz

Lord, help all those who suffer because their fellow men are hard to them. Let them go on believing in human goodness. Let them not become bitter. In spite of everything, let them go on radiating goodness and human kindness. They will be able to do that in you.

Surely everything depends on how we can give meaning to the silence around us.

Laurence Durrell

You are always there, God, with your goodness and love. Let me remember this whenever I feel lonely and deserted, when others do not appreciate me, when they lose patience with me, when they do not talk to me about what interests them, and when no one will listen to me if I have something to say.

You are my God. I can always turn to you. You are always with me, every day of my life. You make life bearable for me. You make me happy.

Whenever I say, think, or do something, I am always happy in the knowledge that you are always present and that you love me.

All around me are people who are inwardly miserable because they have no one to talk to and no one who understands them. They often cease to fight and lose all hope. . . .

But if there is one good person who will listen, that may be enough to provide them with a bridge or way out of their apparently hopeless situation, back to a meaningful existence. *Am I my brother's keeper?*

God, you are no stranger to me. All my life you have been very close to me. Let me continue to trust in your grace. Make me receptive and open to your love. I depend on you entirely. I have nothing else to expect but your love. So stay close to me always.

Care for Me

Care for me, Lord, now that I am old and can no longer fend for myself. The people around me are busy with their own affairs and tend to overlook me. No one seems to understand me and very few people have much time to spare on me. Care for me, Lord.

Give me what I need to eat. Give me clothes and shelter. But also give me a little happiness. Then I shall be able to go on living, however old I become.

Have no anxiety about anything, but in everything, by prayer and supplication with thanksgiving, let your requests be made known to God. And the peace of God, which passes all understanding, will keep your minds in Christ Jesus.

Philippians 4:6-7

Leave all your cares to him who created you. Surely he who thought of you before you existed will care for you now that he has called you into being?

St. Augustine

Three quarters of the cares we have on earth are imaginary.

Meschler

In looking after old people, pastoral care does not have to be the exclusive work of ministers of religion, however necessary they may be in the spiritual care of the aged. It is also the sphere of private initiative. People give pastoral care to each other especially if they are conscious of a shared faith. They can strengthen and support each other.

Cardinal Alfrink

My Longings and Desires

Lord, you know my longings and desires. In my heart, I call for all kinds of things, but only one thing is necessary.

Teach me to be less superficial and to long ardently for the great blessing of union with you. Before this desire is fulfilled, you will quiet my other longings, Lord. *What no eye has seen, nor ear heard, nor the heart of man conceived, what you have prepared for those who love you.*

Let me think of this frequently and look forward now to everything that you are holding in readiness for me.

The best thing that this world can offer is longing for another.

Martin Kessel

One really possesses something most while one still longs for it. In our longing, we experience the object of our longing much more powerfully than we would if we possessed it. As soon as we acquire the object we have wanted so much, almost always we are disillusioned.

Wilhelm von Scholz

Be not afraid when one becomes rich, when the glory of his house increases. For when he dies he will carry nothing away,

his glory will not go after him.
Though, while he lives, he counts
himself happy,
and though a man gets praise when he
does well for himself,
he will go to the generation of his
forefathers
and will never more see the light.
  Man cannot abide in his pomp,
he is like the beasts that perish.

Psalm 49:17-21

Before you leave this world, you must have shown in some way or another your love for Christ.

Matthias Claudius

Nothing should make you afraid and nothing should frighten you. Everything passes. . . . But God remains the same. With patience you will achieve everything. The person who possesses God lacks nothing. Only God satisfies fully.

Teresa of Avila

Inspire me, Holy Spirit,
to think of what is holy.
Impel me, Holy Spirit,
to desire what is holy.
Entice me, Holy Spirit,
to pursue what is holy.
Give me the strength, Holy Spirit,
to hold on to what is holy.
Prevent me, Holy Spirit,
from ever losing it.

St. Augustine

Help me to overcome the need to worry all the time about whether I am pleasing other people or not. Let me just do my best to please You and to take care that You have a good impression of me.

It is clear from their jealousy that people feel very unhappy, and it is clear from the way they always watch what others are doing that they are very bored.

Arthur Schopenhauer

Foolish people are sometimes punished terribly by being fulfilled.

Isolde Kurz

Lord, give me quiet hours in which I can come back to myself. You do not come to me in noise and activity. Fill my quiet hours with your presence.

God is all my hope. I need no other.

Hudson Taylor

Better

I may perhaps know some things better than other people, but I do not act any better. I may be able to manage some things more easily, but I am no more loving than other people. I may possibly achieve more, but do I do more good than others?

Do not let me grumble about others, Lord, or judge them. Let me rather see my own weaknesses.

Let me understand other people, love them, and carry their burdens for them.

Let me see the good in others and let me encourage them to do good by my own good actions.

Being critical does not mean knowing better than others, nor does it mean doing things better yourself. No, being critical means judging correctly, seeing what is good — and that is always difficult — and not just disapproving of what is bad — and that is always very easy.

Ernst Hohenemser

Give me, Lord, a cheerful and patient heart, so that I can be good to everyone I meet. Help me to speak at the right time — and to be silent when silence is necessary. I want to give love in everything I do.

If you want to be good to people, you must overlook a great deal.

Otto Flake

Do not deprive yourself of real joy in life. God wants you to hand on his love. He wants you to love him and all his creatures. And love is the only thing that lasts in time and eternity. If you distribute God's love in this life, heaven begins for you here on earth.

James Keller

No one will ever forgive you for having seen through him — even if he gets away with it.

Arthur Schnitzler

Forgetting oneself by being good to others in little matters — this is what keeps old people alive. It prevents them from becoming self-absorbed. If this happens, old people can become enclosed in themselves and dull and quickly deteriorate.

Paschasius of Marvilde

Experience

I very much need to experience something. I need something to interest me and to make life worth living.

Lord, do not let me be preoccupied simply with appearances. Let me look deeper, below the surface, and experience what lies within.

Let me encounter you, the invisible one, in what is visible and you, the creator, in your creatures.

You can only understand the world insofar as you experience it.

Antione de Saint-Exupéry

It would seem as though everything that I have tried to do has only succeeded so that I should experience it.

Robert Musil

Judging Positively

I want to be positive in my attitude toward life. I do not want to disapprove of everything modern simply because I am no longer young and am not actively involved in life.

I want to see what is good in life today and be glad about it, even if other people are responsible for it.

I do not want to grumble if something is not quite as I would have it. I do not want to be always looking for things that are wrong.

I also want to be honest in my attitude toward what is really bad in the world. If I cannot change it, let me endure it. Perhaps some good will come simply from my good attitude.

Lord, give me patience and do not let me lose my faith in what is good.

Put them all away: anger, wrath, malice, slander and foul talk from your mouth.

Colossians 3:8

Lord, you know how easy it is for the peace that is in us and around us to be destroyed by mistrust, selfishness, and obstinacy. Help us to forgive quickly and to be reconciled with others. Give us your peace. Without you, we shall not know true peace.

The best remedy if you feel yourself getting angry is to wait.

Seneca

May the God of peace himself sanctify you wholly. And may your spirit and soul and body be kept sound and blameless at the coming of our Lord Jesus Christ. He who calls you is faithful and he will do it.

1 Thessalonians 5:23

The man whose judgment is negative cannot be nourished by that judgment.

André Malraux

Do not say everything that you know, but always know everything that you say.

Wilhelm Raabe

There is no uniform Christian pattern of behavior that will never pass out of fashion throughout the centuries. Man is gripped by his own world and, in turn, has a grip on that world. In that situation he is called to use the five or the two talents or the one talent he has been given to extend the place where he is living into a Christian place that will yield a return for the Lord.

Bishop Bekkers

Feeding the Spirit

My spirit has need of food. What I think and whether I can still go on receiving new things — this is really quite important.

Help me, Lord, not to be spiritually lazy and narrow-minded. Do not let me be a know-it-all.

Let me go on seeking and finding the truth that can enrich my spirit.

Do not let my spirit become withered and empty. Protect me from spiritual poverty. I do not want to spend lonely hours thinking of nothing positive.

Let me remain open to your word. In your word, be close to me.

The only solution that people who have very few ideas can find for their problem is to tell those ideas again and again to many different people.

Marquis de Vauvenargues

Lord, give us scientists who are both courageous and humble and who will incorporate the achievements of the modern age into a new Christian vision.

We would lead a fine Christian life if we were less concerned with what others say and do.

Thomas à Kempis

*Teach me, O Lord, the way of thy statutes
and I will keep it to the end.*

*Give me understanding, that I may keep thy law
and observe it with my whole heart. . . .*

*Incline my heart to thy testimonies
and not to gain!*

*Turn my eyes from looking at vanities
and give me life in thy ways.*

Psalm 119:33-34, 36-37

*I delíght to do thy will, O my God.
Thy law is within my heart.*

Psalm 40:8

Let what you say be simply "yes" or "no"; anything more than this comes from evil.

Matthew 3:37

*What man is there who desires life,
and covets many days, that he may enjoy good?*

Keep your tongue from evil
and your lips from speaking deceit.
Depart from evil and do good;
seek peace and pursue it.

Psalm 34:12-14

V. With Each Other and for Each Other

For Married Couples

We have gone through life together and have shared joy and sorrow. We have learned that this life is a great blessing and that your goodness is behind everything. We thank you, Lord.

In all these years we have grown closer and closer together. Now we need each other more than ever.

We wonder, anxiously, which of us will be the first to leave this life. It will be difficult for the one who is left.

But we know that the separation will last only a short time and that we shall see each other again in your kingdom and be happy with each other forever.

Bless our way together and let us take each other to you.

Man is most initimately linked to the one for whom he has sacrificed the most.

E. Hasse

Happy is the man who has a good wife; The number of days that he lives is double.

Sirach 26:1

Happiness in marriage does not depend on whether the partners are similar to each other or quite different in character. What matters is that they are complementary and cannot do without each other.

Love does not die, Paul said. This also applies to love in old age. You could almost say that love does not become old. It is possible to love each other until death, and even beyond death.

If such a beautiful love can continue between two partners who are getting older, their old age also will be beautiful. Their love will continue to radiate warmth, though not in the same way it did in their younger days. Then it was the first glimmer of light in the morning. Now it is the warm glow of evening sunset. Then it was the blossoming of early spring. Now it is the full ripeness of a beautiful autumn.

Alois Stiefvater

My husband and I have often talked to each other about the meaning of death and the life that follows it. Both of us were certain that death is the gateway to eternal life, and so we promised each other that the color of our funeral rite would be white.

Queen Wilhelmina

My wife and I, hand in hand, are approaching our eighties. We are living quietly and peacefully in the evening of our life. Every day is a feast day.

We never thought that it would be sad to get old. On the contrary, we quite looked forward to it. We had our fair share of sorrow and adversity. Our fair share, yes, but we also experienced a great deal of happiness. We thank God for both.

Now we are living in the happiest days of our life. We can look back to our past and see only what was good and beautiful in it. Only silly people say that it is sad to be old. Calmly and quietly, we look forward to the end of our life. Our grave is waiting for us — one grave for the two of us. On the stone will be the words: *Deus est amor,* God is love.

Ernest Claes

For the Children

Lord, you gave us children. We had to go to a great deal of trouble looking after them, but they have brought us great happiness.

You gave us watchfulness so that we could watch over them, tenderness so that we could love them, wisdom so that we could guide them, and patience so that we could wait until they were old enough to go their own way.

Now they are more your children than ours. Bless them.

When your son has grown up, become his brother.

Arab proverb

May the Lord, Almighty God, bless you. May he shower blessings on you. May you see your grandchildren into the third and fourth generations and be happy in your old age.

Marriage blessing

Parents find it most difficult to overlook faults in their children that they have learned themselves.

Marie von Ebner-Eschenbach

In the pastoral care of people who are getting older, it is important to watch out for isolation, a withdrawal into the stronghold of earlier, familiar patterns of life. There is no need to annoy older people with all kinds of novelties that make them feel ill at ease, but it is important to prevent them from becoming alienated from the Church, which is developing so quickly and is the Church of their children and grandchildren. But it is also the Church with which they want to go on being associated.

Cardinal Alfrink

For the Grandchildren

Lord, you have given me grandchildren and this is a source of great happiness.

I can share their little cares and sympathize with them when they are upset or want something. They brighten the whole of my life.

Protect them and let me go on experiencing happiness in them.

Children are a bridge to heaven.

Proverb

No child really likes being a child, but when we are old it is wonderful to look back at the time when we were still children.

Cesare Pavese

Young people often have a very difficult time. They run great risks. They are open to everything, but it is not easy for them to distinguish between truth and appearances, sincerity and deceit. Protect them, Lord, and look after them.

Let them be innocent and happy, cheerful and full of thanks. Give them good friends. Friendship will make them open to life. Help them to look for what is good and to find you.

When we are young, we all think that the world began with us and that everything is there only for us.

Goethe

Although I often have to smile, a little indulgently, about the spontaneous, boisterous behavior of the young people around me, I can still try to help them build a world fit for people to live in.

What I must not do is be selfish and cold and withdraw into isolation. I must go on taking a lively interest in life around me.

For My Family and Acquaintances

You have given me people, Lord, to belong to me in some way or another, people with whom I can live, people who know me, people with whom I am acquainted.

It is fine to know good people with whom I can talk, people who don't let me down, people who are good to me.

Although I often find it difficult to be patient with other people, to put up with them and always be ready to listen to them or help them, I still thank you for my family and my acquaintances.

It is strange how your nearest and dearest are often the people you find least easy to get on with. Don't worry — it is often the same with them.

Feuchtersleben

Whether or not a house is a home depends on the people who live in it.

Weismantel

Bless the members of my family, Lord, and my acquaintances. Let what they do be fruitful. Let them be successful and be happy in their success. Let them also be sensible and good.

If they have little time for prayer, let me pray instead. If you are good to us, we shall be good to each other.

For the Christian no man is a stranger. Anyone we meet and above all the person who most needs our help is at once our neighbor.

It does not matter whether he is a member of our family or not, whether we like him or not or whether he deserves our help or not.

Edith Stein

The whole of our life we look for extraordinary people, instead of seeing the ordinary people around us as extraordinary.

Hans Urs von Balthasar

For Friends

It is wonderful to have friends — people who understand me, who are well disposed toward me, who are sympathetic when I am happy or sad, who spare time for me.

Let me, then, give to my friends as well as receive from them.

Let me show interest and not just expect it. Let me devote time to them and try to make their lives happier.

There is only one way of overcoming loneliness: by loving. Love breaks through all barriers and can penetrate to even the loneliest heart, so long as that heart is open.

Reinhold Schneider

We expect other people always to be ready to treat us with interest. We should therefore not limit our interest in them to occasional moments.

In this question of interest, there are always two people involved. One receives interest and thus gains. The other gives and thus loses.

It is, however, possible for both to gain. This happens when both give equally. It is even possible for one to gain simply by giving, especially when he does not even expect the other to give.

Wolfgana Trillhaas

You can only be certain of a friend when everything around you is uncertain.

Ennius

Lord, you have given me the great good fortune of a friend, someone whom I understand and who understands me. This friendship is more valuable to me than all the riches in the world.

Help us to understand each other better. Stay with us. Then we shall be able to take each other to you.

Inspire us with the right words when the other is happy or sad. Do not let us be selfish. Do not let one of us feel better than the other.

Thank you, Lord, for letting me have someone whom I understand and who understands me.

You are not at home where you happen to live. Home is the place where you are understood.

Christian Morgenstern

Each person is a deep mystery to everyone else. What is strange is that they can ever become friends.

Otto Michel

We all need someone who is good to us, both at home and outside. We need a friend who understands us and is concerned for us — someone who will stay with us when times are difficult. We need someone, too, for whom we can do something. We too need to show concern for someone.

Make us capable, Lord, of giving and receiving friendship like this. You showed us your own goodness and love of mankind in your Son. He became our brother. He gave his life for us. He will not forsake us now. Let us love each other too, with all our heart.

Friends speak frankly to each other.
They share each other's thoughts and worries.
They teach each other
    and learn from each other.
They give to each other
    and receive from each other.
They pour out for each other
    and drink with each other.

Aelred of Rievaulx

For Neighbors

It is a great blessing to have good neighbors. I can have a good chat with them, hear their news, and tell them about myself. They are sympathetic when I am going through a bad time. We can depend on each other and help each other. I like them very much.

Lord, help us go on being good neighbors.

In our great cities, less than 50 percent of old people know their neighbors. About 84 percent do no more than wish each other the time of day. They know nothing about each other's financial situation. They do not know how their neighbors are getting on. They have no idea of each other's difficulties. Ought we not to be doing something about this great indifference, this distance between people?

On the other hand, of course, are many people who value this distance between themselves and their neighbors. Good neighbors are a blessing, but even though we may have people living next door, above us, or beneath us, this does not mean we have friendly relationships with them.

It is more important for us to have people living near us on whom we can rely when we really need them, rather than people who tend to intrude on us. We must also accept the fact that neighbors do not always respond to our invitations. That may be human kindness. Keeping one's distance is not always indifference. People are different from each other.

Maybe their behavior does not please me. I must not be narrow-minded or critical. Let me accept that they are different. I must not be proud and obstinate. I must not refuse to make concessions in the cause of peace.

Lord, help me to take into account the differences between me and my fellow men — their character, their peculiarities and their shortcomings. They also must often have to overlook aspects of *my* character.

Love is patient and kind; love is not jealous or boastful; it is not arrogant or rude. Love does not insist on its own way; it is not irritable or resentful; it does not rejoice at wrong, but rejoices in the right. Love bears all things, believes all things, hopes all things, endures all things.

1 Corinthians 13:4-7

The good man is not only warm and friendly toward others. He also simply accepts that others have good intentions.

Maurice Blondel

Sailing or drifting in thick mist, the admiral or the commander of the fleet should order a cannon to fire every hour or every two bells so that the ships will stay together more easily.

Naval instruction, 1673

Everyone Is My Neighbor

I want to go forward to meet everyone with the right attitude. I want to listen attentively to what each person I meet has to say to me and be thankful that he or she is warm and friendly.

Let me too, Lord, be warm and friendly toward others, so that they will feel at ease with me, know that I am always ready to help them or be helped by them, and realize that I am patient and understanding with them, especially if they are young. Let me be sensitive to other people's difficulties.

I thank you, Lord, that you want me to be a good person and that you have surrounded me with good people. I also thank you because you seem to need me to do things for you.

If I sometimes feel lonely and have the impression that life is going on without me, let me be comforted by the thought that you are always with me.

The person who can listen attentively, ask sensible questions, reply calmly, and be silent when he has nothing else to say has the qualities that are most needed in life.

Johann K. Lavater

Should the person who cannot speak perhaps be able to listen well?

Ludwig Hohl

What does the man who has never suffered really know about life?

Henry Suso

God, you support me and I can hold on to you. How fantastic it is, your presence in my life. I cannot keep it to myself. I have to say it openly and thank you for it.

God is present in my life and he is good. He is good and merciful. He holds on to us when we are afraid of falling. He sets us on our feet when we feel hopeless and want to let things slide. He is our light when everything is dark all around us. He is always

there when we call out to him. He
hears our cry and comes to help us.

God, you support me and I can hold
on to you. How fantastic it is, your
presence in my life. You protect all
those who love you. You look for those
who trust you. You help all those who
hope in you.

When I do not know how to carry on,
when I do not know what to do next —
at such times I look for you. You
support me then and I can hold on to
you. How fantastic it is, you presence
in my life.

                    Severin Schneider

Lord, give me the gift
to change
what can be changed. . . .
   Give me the patience
to endure
what cannot be changed. . . .
   Give me enough understanding
to be able to distinguish
one from the other.

                    Anton Kner

Blind people remain blind
until someone gets up
and goes over to them,
until someone comes
and sees for them.

Dumb people remain dumb
until someone gets up
and goes over to them,
until someone comes
and speaks for them.

Deaf people remain deaf
until someone gets up
and goes over to them,
until someone comes
and hears for them.

Dead people remain dead
until someone gets up
and goes over to them,
until someone comes
and lives for them.

It takes a man two years to learn how
to talk and fifty years to learn how to
keep silent.

Ernest Hemingway

God gave man two ears but only one tongue, so that he could listen twice as well as he could speak.

Arab proverb

You know how much trouble can be caused if you insist on telling the truth to people. Surely we ought to value prudence and love of our neighbor higher. These are not always served by telling the truth!

Bishop Bekkers

For the Sick

Lord, give our sick friends and relatives patience. For them, every day is a long period of waiting. They wait for the doctor, for people to help them, and for the return of good health. Be with them, Lord, so that their illness will be beneficial for them.

Lord, give them trust. Their thoughts go back again and again to their own troubles. Let them also experience something that is good. Send people to them who will listen to them and comfort them, people who will show them that they are loved. Be with them yourself, Lord, so that they will gain strength from your love.

If we were not ill sometimes, would our lives be really healthy?

Emil Gött

In God I am happy and contented. I accept everything that he sends me, both pleasant and unpleasant, with thanks. He knows what is best for us. That is why I am always happy, in God.

Conrad of Parzham

When we have been ill, we cannot get better until we have been made better by our illness.

Rittelmeyer

For Those Who Are Gravely Ill

Lord, help those who are gravely ill.

The meaning of suffering is not always clear to us, but we firmly believe that you can always bring something good out of it. You make sure that suffering makes people grow inwardly.

Help those who have to contend with serious illness and who have no certain prospect of recovery. Help them come to terms with their problem. Send people to them who will be good to them and who, by their goodness and warmth, will make their almost unbearable suffering lighter.

Perhaps, also, they will find you, Lord, in their suffering. They can still give meaning to their existence in prayer and sacrifice. You love everyone who follows you on the way of the cross, like you, accepts the Father's will. So, Lord, you will certainly support all who are gravely ill.

Almighty, eternal God,
the salvation of those who believe in you,
hear our prayer for your sick friends.

We ask you urgently
to be merciful to them
and to restore their health.

Then they will, with this community,
be able to praise and thank you again.

Liturgical prayer

*Take the trouble to visit a sick man. You
will be loved in return.*

Sirach 7:35

For the Dying

At every moment of the day — at this
very moment — many people are
dying. Again and again, someone we
know dies. Not far from where we live
are hospitals in which people are
dying. On our roads, people lose their
lives every moment of the day.

Lord, have mercy on the dying. They
are often afraid to die. Sometimes
they have to suffer a great deal before
they die.

Help them, Lord, to appreciate the
seriousness of their situation. Help

them to take their leave of the world —
their place in it and the people and
things they love — in the knowledge
that they will be able to be happy with
you.

Give them the strength to put right
what has gone wrong in their family
life, their personal life, their life with
other people, and their life with you.

Give them understanding, Lord.
Make them happy in the knowledge
that you love us all and that in you we
find fulfillment.

*If we live, we live to the Lord and, if we
die, we die to the Lord; so, then,
whether we live or whether we die, we
are the Lord's.*

Romans 14:8

Help us, Lord, to live every moment of
the day as though it were eternity. We
cannot imagine what the hereafter is
like — our thoughts are too
earthbound. But you show us what
leads to eternal life. Give us the
strength, Lord, to do it.

It is a sign of God's mercy that man does not know when he will die. He must therefore live every day well, since the day of his dying is hidden from him.

St. Augustine

For Invalids and Disabled People

Man attaches great value to physical health, but not everyone has a perfect body. Many people have physical defects that make life difficult for them.

Let me be sympathetic and understanding when I meet such people. Give me sufficient love, Lord, so that I am as open and free with them as with everyone else.

Let me also go beyond their outward appearance, Lord, and discover the inner value and goodness of their soul.

Let me recognize, Lord, that something is required of me when I encounter an invalid or a disabled fellow man. I must in some way help him carry his cross. I must serve him as well as I can.

You love all who are poor, sick, handicapped, and suffering. Let me encounter you in them.

Jesus said: "Go and tell John what you hear and see: the blind receive their sight and the lame walk, lepers are cleansed and the deaf hear. The dead are raised up and the poor have good news preached to them."

Matthew 11:4-5

About two-thirds of all people over the age of sixty-five find walking difficult. Seventy-five percent of those over seventy have difficulty walking.

The blind and the lame came to him in the temple and he healed them.

Matthew 21:14

Pope John XXIII once visited a children's hospital. Among the patients, most of whom would soon be well enough to go home, was twelve-year-old Silvio Colagrande, who could now see again as the result of a cornea transplant. Don Gnocchi, a priest, had been his donor. Silvio told the pope: "I am seeing with Don Gnocchi's eyes."

In the next bed was a boy who had got lime in his eyes while he was playing. The pope tried to comfort him and said a donor might be found for him too: "There are so many good people." The pope was moved to tears.

He came to the bed of a seven-year-old girl, Carmin Gemma, who had become blind two or three month previously as a result of meningitis. As the pope came to her, she said: "I know you are the pope, but I can't see you."

John sat on the edge of the bed and held her little hands in his. He did not speak for some time. Then he said, as if he were thinking aloud: "We are all often blind."

For Those Who Are Disappointed

Everyone is disappointed at some time or another. You were looking forward to something and it turned out quite differently from what you had expected. There were all kinds of reasons for it, but you have to accept the fact that this is what happened.

Lord, do not let me be so eager to achieve what I want. Let your will be done in my life. Prevent me from becoming unreasonable in my disappointment and making others suffer because of it.

Help all people who are disappointed to accept their sorrow and to be comforted by your love, in the knowledge that you will never abandon them.

Be our consolation, Lord, when we ourselves feel disappointed.

It is absurd to be sad about something that proved not to be lasting. If it disappeared, it disappeared because it was not capable of lasting.

Paul Ernst

174

My neighbor is not the man or woman whom I like or love the most, but the one who most needs me.

Queen Wilhelmina

For Those We Cannot Reach

There are so many people who have given up trying. They may perhaps give the impression of being friendly and helpful, but now and then they give us a glimpse of their true attitude. They seem to be dead within. They live in the night. They cannot be reached. They feel abandoned by God and man. No prayer comes from their heart. There is no hope. All that they seem to have is a longing that is painful because it is disappointed.

We must pray for those people. This means that we must pray their prayer for them, hope their hope for them, go into the night in order to be with them.

Save me, O God!
for the waters have come up to my neck.

I sink in the deep mire,
*   where there is no foothold;*
I have come into deep waters,
*   and the flood sweeps over me.*
I am weary with my crying;
*   my throat is parched.*
My eyes grow dim
*   with waiting for my God. . . .*
But my prayer is to thee, O Lord.
At an acceptable time, O God,
*   in the abundance of thy steadfast*
love answer me.
With thy faithful help rescue me from
sinking in the mire;
*   let me be delivered from my enemies*
*   and from the deep waters.*
Let not the flood sweep over me
*   or the deep swallow me up.*

Psalm 69:1-4, 14-16

Lord, I pray for those who cannot pray any more themselves because they have lost hope and lack the strength to forget the past.

Perhaps they have never been able to love themselves. Perhaps they cannot forget their unhappy

childhood. Perhaps they still grieve
about opportunities they have missed
or never had. Perhaps they are unable
to forgive themselves for some
stupidity they committed, an action
they think was disastrous in their
lives. Perhaps they were once very
happy and, when the moment of
happiness passed, have never, they
think, been happy since.

Lord, I pray for those who cannot
pray any more themselves because
they cannot find the words, because
they feel that they no longer belong to
our world or because they think that
you or we can no longer reach them.
You must be able to find them
somewhere, Lord. If they cannot find
you, then you will certainly go out to
meet them in the night.

I ask you this, Lord, because I know
only too well how empty life can
sometimes seem.

*The Spirit helps us in our weakness, for
we do not know how to pray as we
ought, but the Spirit himself intercedes
for us with sighs too deep for words.*

*And he who searches the hearts of men
knows what is the mind of the Spirit,
because the Spirit intercedes for the
saints according to the will of God.*

Romans 8: 26-27

For Annoying People

There are so many annoying people,
Lord. They irritate others by what they
say and do. Help them, Lord.
Give them patience, Lord, if their
nerves fail them.
Give them love if they insist inflexibly
on their rights.
Give them peace if they are upset.
Give them magnanimity if others
cannot cope with them.
Give them happiness if they feel low.
Give them someone to whom they can
talk openly.
Give them sufficient understanding of
themselves and others, so that they
do not always blame others for everything.
Give them the courage to admit their
own faults.

Give them deep faith in you. Then they will change in their attitude toward you and us.

Be concerned for each other. Nothing is more important than that. Do not grumble about bad times when you hear others doing it. God needs you here and now and he gives you strength here and how.

Alfred Bengsch

If one has a complaint against another, forgive each other. As the Lord has forgiven you, so you also must forgive.

Colossians 3:13

No quarrel would last very long if only one person was in the wrong.

La Rochefoucauld

Little children, let us not love in word and speech, but in deed and truth.

1 John 3:18

We are often consoled by a mere trifle, because we let a mere trifle upset us.

Blaise Pascal

The man who stands on his toes will not remain upright for very long.

Each Other's Burden's

I know very many people who are often a real burden to others. But we have been given the task of bearing each other's burdens.

I want to do that, Lord, out of love. Show me, then, how to do it — when I feel uncomfortable in the presence of such people, when their behavior upsets me, when their selfishness repels me, when I am hurt by their constant fault-finding.

Help me, Lord, to endure such people and, what is more, to love them, since that is what you want.

There is probably only one way of finding a thing, an animal, or another human being really beautiful — you have to love.

Robert Musil

The worst sin that we can commit against our fellow man is not to hate him, but to be indifferent towards him.

George Bernard Shaw

Lord, let me be patient with people who are physically or spiritually handicapped. Help me to endure their misfortunes.

Let me trust people who have been in prison or who are held in one way or another in suspicion. Help me overcome my prejudices.

Let me be tactful in what I say to people who are distressed and help me to console them in the right way.

Help me to love the sick and to bring a little light into their lives.

Help me, too, be gentle with all the people I meet and to treat them as you want me too.

How often it must have happened that someone who was deeply hurt lacked a little genuine Christian love at the decisive moment in his life.

Edzard Schaper

It is always worthwhile taking on a heavy burden if you can make life a little lighter for one other person.

Stefan Zweig

We Are All Weak

Let me endure the annoyances caused by other people, Lord. We are all weak. Other people often have to put up with me when I am annoying.

Do not let me give too much attention to the weaknesses of other people. If I do, I only hurt myself.

I need a great deal of patience and goodness, especially now that I am getting old.

Make me patient and good, then, Lord, so that I shall be able to endure

difficult, annoying people and so that something good will come from my contact with them.

Be merciful, even as your Father is merciful.
Judge not, and you will not be judged.
Condemn not, and you will not be condemned.
Forgive, and you will be forgiven.
Give, and it will be given to you;
good measure, pressed down, shaken together, running over. . . .
For the measure you give will be the measure you get back.

Luke 6:36-38

There are two ways of doing good: giving away and forgiving. Giving away what you have been given and forgiving what has been done to you.

St. Augustine

You went to a great deal of trouble, Lord, to save us. You let yourself be crucified to set us free.

You took so much on yourself. I find it so difficult to let anything happen to me without protesting.

Help me, Lord, not to reply sharply to a sharp comment. Help me not to hurt others when they hurt me.

We are always ready to believe evil of others rather than good and to speak about it. How I wish that I had more often held my tongue!

Thomas à Kempis

To have the courage to admit that one was wrong is a great step forward. It shows a feeling for truth and a genuine attitude.

Bishop Bekkers

Wholehearted Forgiveness

I can so easily overlook my own faults, but I am relentless where others are concerned.

Let me learn something of your goodness and loving kindness, Lord, and help me to be tolerant and to forgive others wholeheartedly.

I expect others to be loving and indulgent where I am concerned, but I am so hard and so slow to forgive.

Let me learn from your cross. Let me be hard toward myself and kind to others.

Be a man of prayer and you will also be a man of peace.

Leon Bloy

Why do you see the speck in your brother's eye, but do not notice the log that is in your own eye? Or how can you say to your brother, "Let me take the speck out of your eye," when there is a log in your own eye? You hypocrite, first take the log out of your own eye and then you will see clearly to take the speck out of your brother's eye.

Matthew 7:3-5

We disapprove of little shortcomings in others, but never talk about our own faults.

Thomas à Kempis

Do not wait before you forgive; it saves time and is good for the digestion.

O'Connell

VI. The Day is Drawing to a Close

You and I

You and I
belong together —
you, Lord,
because you have loved me
and want to make me happy forever;
I,
because I need you,
cannot do without you,
and know that everything else
is empty and meaningless.
You and I
will together be happy forever —
you, Lord,
because you have loved without
reserve;
I,
because I am loved without reserve.

I might have been a saint. And what
did I become? A writer.... I have
written a few pages that people have
admired. But they do not know that it is

just the residue or sediment of a great vocation that I have made an atrocious mess of and of which God will ask me to give an account.

I have always been on the lookout for what I wanted from God and never for what he wanted from me. And here I am now, sixty-eight years old and nothing to show but a few sheets of paper with scribble on them.

Léon Bloy

You should not be too worried if it suddenly seems as though everything that you have ever thought about God is wrong and that God does not really exist. That is something that happens to very many people.

What you must not think is that you really no longer believe in the existence of God. If you are no longer able to believe in God in the way in which you did in the past, that is because you did not believe then in quite the right way. It is best, in such circumstances, to think seriously about what you really mean by God. . . .

If a primitive man ceases to believe in his wooden god, that does not mean that God does not exist. All that it means is that the true God is not a piece of wood.

Leo Tolstoi

Thank You for Faith

Lord, thank you for founding the Church and letting me feel secure in it.

Thank you, Lord, for the people who are concerned about my salvation and who help me on my way to you.

Thank you for giving us your word and for being the way, the truth, and the life.

Thank you for being there and for being so great and admirable. You are beyond my understanding, Lord. Even though I cannot comprehend you, I can still love you and belong to you.

Thank you for being my God and for wanting to receive us in your eternal blessedness. That is why we can bear what we still have to bear here on earth.

Thank you, Lord, for having created me.

Religion begins where there is every reason to cease being religious.

Joseph Bernhart

The more concerned you are with life, the more concerned you should be with religion.

George Bernard Shaw

If you separate the world from God, it becomes too heavy for one man.

Karl Pfleger

Some people simply believe
  and raise up their hearts to the Lord.

Some do not seek status or possessions,
  but serve God all their lives.

Some keep the Lord's commandments
  and pray without ceasing.

Some work to please God
  and do not expect a reward.

Some offer their lives up to God
  and imitate his Son on the cross.

Some are the salt of the earth
  or a light shining before men.

Keep them all, Lord, and protect them.

A. J. D. van Oosten

The Power of Prayer

The less work I do, the more I can pray
and be spiritually active. Some people
drive themselves unmercifully until
they drop. But everything ultimately
depends on you, Lord. If you do not
build the house, we, the workers, labor
in vain.

    Accept my prayer, Lord. It comes
from my heart. You are at the center of
my life.

When his prayer became more intense
and ardent, he found that he had much

less to say. Finally, he became quite silent in prayer. He became silent and — there is really no greater contrast to speaking — he began to listen.

He had first believed that prayer was speaking. But then he discovered that prayer was keeping silent and more than this — it was listening.

And that it what it is — not listening to yourself speaking, but being quiet until you hear God.

Sören Kierkegaard

Many people could become saints if they devoted as much time and energy to their inner growth as they do to earning money, and if they spent only part of the effort they spend on pleasing people in the world to serving God.

Julius Langbein

If a man prays
as well as he can,
his prayer will be powerful —
a bitter heart is made sweet,

a sad heart happy,
a poor heart rich,
a silly heart wise,
an anxious heart brave,
a weak heart strong,
a blind heart seeing,
a cool heart ardent. . . .
    For prayer brings God down
into our little hearts
and takes our hearts up
to God, the source of all life.
    It brings together
two lovers—
God and the soul.

Gertrude the Great

When we pray we should pray above
all for others. This kind of prayer will
give new depth to our lives and enrich
our minds.
    All our life we have worked for
others. Now we are older and cannot
do much more for them. But we can
still pray — for our children and
grandchildren, our friends and

acquaintances, and for our dear ones
who have gone before us in the sign of
faith.

Alois Stiefvater

I Belong to You

You think of me — I am quite sure of
this.

Of course, we live in a hard world
where there is a great deal of
suffering. Every day we hear of
terrible natural disasters. Yet I still
believe that the world is governed by a
higher power and that our lives have a
higher purpose.

You are the Lord and creator of our
world. Everything is in your hands,
including man. You are our Father and
you love us.

I am glad about this and I thank you
for being the center, the point around
which everything turns. I thank you too
for being my future. I can trust in your
love.

We can only acquire the things that are eternal by sacrificing some of our time and being prepared to wait for them.

Aldous Huxley

Prayer is a way of justifying our existence.

Georges Bernanos

It is not so bad when people seem to be distracted in church. What happens there transcends the senses and they may grasp it better this way than by trying very hard to understand it intellectually.

Christian Morgenstern

Turning Back to God

There must be many people who are hardly able to say exactly when and how they have sinned and in what ways they have been unjust to others.

So it is perhaps better to ask a

different question. When have I let matters rest? When have I not lived as I know I should? When have I behaved as though God had never called me?

Then I must ask why. Why have I acted that way? Because I wanted to take things easy? Because I was afraid? Because I was seeking my own interests? Because I was feeling irresponsible? Because I did not think of society, but only myself? Or was it because of unconscious inhibitions that were too vague for me to define?

Why have I not behaved as I felt called to behave? That is the central question that I must ask myself in the depths of my heart and my conscience.

To hear God's call and respond to it lovingly and effectively — that is the great challenge that confronts us today.

Friedrich von Gagern

God, almighty Father, you are the Lord of my life. Nothing is hidden from you. You have called me to look critically at my own life in your presence.

Your Son, Jesus Christ, has given me an example in his life of how I ought to do your will. I was baptized in his name, and because of him I am a Christian. I will therefore measure everything that I think, say or do by what he thought, said, and did.

Through your Holy Spirit enlighten my understanding and let me examine my faults and shortcomings. Move me to admit my sins and be sorry for them. Give me the strength to improve. Amen.

We are never finished with ourselves. . . .

Again and again, as long as we live, we are confronted with our own faults and weaknesses. Man's life is always a struggle. It is only at the end of time that we shall find fulfillment.

As creatures, we need not be ashamed of having to turn inward again and again in humility to examine our conscience. And we should not be angry, but very thankful whenever someone who loves us makes us aware of our own faults.

We ought not be sad that we are getting older and yet still finding out that we are doing the same wrong things that we did when we were young. The points at which we examine our conscience are often the same for a very long time.

That should not prevent our giving an account of ourselves again and again and asking God to forgive us and help us.

Robert Svoboda

Put on, then, as God's chosen ones, holy and beloved, compassion, kindness, lowliness, meekness and patience, forbearing one another and, if one has a complaint against the other, forgiving each other; as the Lord has

*forgiven you, so you also must forgive.
And above all put on love, which binds
everything together in perfect harmony.*

*And let the peace of Christ rule in
your hearts, to which indeed you were
called in one body. And be thankful.*

*Let the word of Christ dwell in you
richly, as you teach and admonish one
another in all wisdom.... And
whatever you do, in word or deed, do
everything in the name of the Lord
Jesus, giving thanks to God the Father
through him.*

Colossians 3:12-17

**God, turning away from you means
falling,
turning toward you means standing up
again,
remaining in you means having firm
ground under one's feet. . . .**

**God, leaving you means dying, go-
ing back to you means being reborn,
dwelling in you means living.**

St. Augustine

It is not good for us spiritually to stare
too long at our failures. We all prefer
to look at what has succeeded rather
than at what has failed in our lives.
Although we should not stare at what
has gone wrong, it makes a good
mirror for self-criticism, which ought to
be used regularly. So long as we don't
spend the whole day looking at it!

P. A. van Stempvoort

The Bible and Spiritual Reading

Reading spiritual books helps to
deepen and enrich our personal
spiritual life. It is not, strictly speaking,
a form of study directed toward
acquiring knowledge. The aim is to
help us become more faithful
Christians and better people. What we
read should have an effect on our
hearts and orientate us toward
*righteousness, faith, love and peace,
along with all those who call upon the
Lord from a pure heart* (2 Timothy
2:22).

Reading of this kind acts like gentle rain on plants, making us grow. The most important book for spiritual reading is the Bible. The most important part of the Bible for Christians is the New Testament and, in the New Testament, the Gospels.

Continue in what you have learned and have firmly believed, knowing from whom you learned it and how from childhood you have been acquainted with the sacred writings which are able to instruct you for salvation through faith in Christ Jesus. All scripture is inspired by God and profitable for teaching, for reproof, for correction and for training in righteousness, that the man of God may be complete, equipped for every good work.

2 Timothy 3:14-17

**Make an effort every day to consider the words of the Creator.
Get to know the heart of God from his Word.**

Gregory the Great

In spiritual reading, a good method is to meditate on a passage or a story. There are many possibilities: a piece from one of the gospels or epistles, a prayer, a passage from a book you have just read.

Read it through quietly. Perhaps the word "read" is wrong here. You *read* a newspaper, but you *experience* something that is particularly beautiful or that goes deeper. Try, then, to penetrate to the spirit of what you are "reading." Meditate on it, not in your intellect but in your heart.

A favorite way of doing this — it has been popular for centuries — is to read, pray, and contemplate. Begin by reading a psalm or some other suitable passage from the Bible. Try to experience the warmth of God's Spirit behind the words themselves. Taste the Spirit in the words, like a bee tasting nectar in a flower. Stay still. The reading will then, of its own accord, become prayer. You will spontaneously turn toward God. As you remain quiet and prayerful, you will begin to contemplate and rest in God.

J. van Rooy

Do not read too much at a time. It should not be a downpour, but a steady, slow, and penetrating rain.

F. X. Mutz

People will better get to know Christ, the bringer of our salvation, and love him more ardently and imitate him more faithfully, as they know and consider Scripture, and especially the New Testament. In the words of St. Jerome, ignorance of Scripture is ignorance of Christ.

Pius XII

What is the heart of the gospel message? It is that God is so human in Jesus Christ that he speaks to us on our own wavelength. Jesus Christ says: *Who has seen me has seen the Father.*

P. A. van Stempvoort

St. Paul tells us, *the letter kills, but the Spirit gives life.* A man has been killed by the letter when he wants to know quotations only so that people will think he is very learned. A religious has been killed by the letter when he has no desire to follow the spirit of Holy Scripture, but wants to know what it says only so that he can explain it to others. On the other hand, those have received life from the spirit of Sacred Scripture who, by their words and example, refer to the most high God, to whom belongs all good, all that they know or wish to know, and do not allow their knowledge to become a source of self-complacency.

St. Francis of Assisi

Jesus must have been unforgettable and fascinating. He belonged completely to his people, living in the harsh land of Palestine, but at the same time he was also quite different. He was a striking figure. He was a stumbling block. He surprised some people, and others admired him. That

is very clear from the gospels.
Everywhere, people whispered and
talked about him. Rumors were rife.
He was always surrounded by a
crowd. People were always thinking
about him, his words and deeds.

We know from our own experience
what that means. Anyone who is well
known or important in any way, or has
some power of attraction or authority,
always makes us feel uneasy.
Associating with such a person makes
us reflect about ourselves. It was the
same with Jesus. He makes us feel
that something is taking place in our
lives. He urges us to imitate his
example.

Bishop Bekkers

Have you a Bible? Or at least a New
Testament? If you haven't, buy one or
get someone to give you one. Then
read it every day, if only for a short
time. Do not study it critically. Just
read it as an ordinary person would
read it if he wants to hear what God
has to say to him.

Just open it and begin to read. . .
until something strikes you — a word,
a sentence, or a passage that speaks
to your soul quite personally. Then
close the book and think about the
piece you have just read. You will find
that God's word can often be very
appropriate.

Alois Stiefvater

Meditation

Meditation or interior prayer brings
the spirit and heart of man into
personal contact with God.

When you think about God or the
great truths of faith, you are led to
express your faith, hope, and love and
are consequently made to pray.
Sometimes, however, that faith, hope,
love, or prayer can arise spontaneously in you, without any prompting,
and make you turn to God.

This experience is known as
meditation or interior prayer. It is an
inner fire that illuminates and
strengthens, gives peace, and heals
the soul.

The best point of departure for meditation is a reading from the Bible. There are other such points, however, such as the beauty of God's creation, a simple flower, a religious picture, or a photograph of someone we love.

The center of our meditation is always God. Through meditation, he can become the center of our life.

You prayed alone on a mountain
and, Jesus, I can find no mountain
high enough to climb and find you.
The world is always following me —
wherever I go,
wherever I look.
There is no man
as poor as I am,
none who suffers such need
and cannot complain,
none so hungry
and cannot ask,
not one in such pain
and cannot express it!
O Lord, help me, poor fool that I am,
to pray to you.

Guido Gezelle

The flowers speak to me,
the plants address me;
everything that God has made
greets me every day.

                              Guido Gezelle

To see the world in a grain of sand,
    and heaven in a wild flower;
Hold
infinity in the palm of your hand,
    and
eternity in an hour.

                              William Blake

You may ask, how should I meditate
and on what should I meditate? It may
have happened that a picture made a
tremendous impression on you at
some time in your life. You can use
that picture or a reproduction of it for
meditation.
    You should not, of course, look at it
as you would at those in an illustrated
magazine, flicking through the pages
and not really considering any one
picture, but always looking ahead to
the next.

The most suitable is a religious picture: Jesus' birth, Jesus carrying his cross, the empty tomb, and so on. Sit in front of it, look at it attentively, receive it completely into yourself, and then let your thoughts be liberated.

They will always be good thoughts — a kind of prayer — and very suitable for older people.

Alois Stiefvater

Dying

Very few people know what to do or think about dying or death. They do not like thinking about it.

Yet we ought to think seriously about it, since it is the last experience that we shall undergo and it is extremely important.

Before we die, we want to put various things right with regard to God and our fellow men. Death can take us by surprise, and the chance may be lost.

Above all, we should not forget that we cannot escape death. On the other hand, there have been many opportunities in life to experience God's love, and we can be sure that he will not desert us when we come to die. We know that this life will be taken from us, but we also believe firmly that a new and better life is waiting for us.

It is therefore very important for us to begin to prepare ourselves for death. We should try — now — to accept the fact of dying and death from God's hands. We do not know whether we shall die suddenly or whether we shall be so ill at the end that we are hardly conscious of what is happening to us.

So we should pray regularly *now:* Lord, I accept death from your hands, whenever it may come and in whatever way it comes. I accept it with all its fear, pain, and sadness. I am full of trust, because I know I shall rise again and live in you. Whoever believes in you will live, even though he has to die.

We would not have you ignorant, brethren, concerning those who are asleep, that you may not grieve as others do who have no hope. For since we believe that Jesus died and rose again, even so, through Jesus, God will bring with him those who have fallen asleep ... and so we shall always be with the Lord.

1 Thessalonians 4:13-15, 17

You Are Always the Same

Everything changes — everything around me and even my own heart. Hardly a day goes by but I notice some changes, and of course it has its effect on me. Nothing remains the same. Even our happiest experiences must pass.
What have I to look forward to? I cannot control the future. I do not know what is going to happen. I do not even know how long I shall live.

What should I hold on to? On whom can I rely, if not on you? You are always the same, Lord. It is only from you that I can expect salvation.

Our expectation of fulfillment at the end of time means that our present sufferings must be regarded as temporary. We know too that they contain a promise. "If we are children of God, we are also heirs, heirs of God and fellow heirs with Christ, provided we suffer with him in order that we may also be glorified with him. I consider," said the apostle Paul, "that the sufferings of the present time are not worth comparing with the glory that is to be revealed to us" (Romans 17-18).

Hans Küng

*Lord, let me know my end
and what is the measure of my days;
let me know how fleeting my life is!
   Behold, thou hast made my days a
few handbreadths,
and my lifetime is nothing in thy sight.
   Surely every man stands as a mere
breath!
Surely man goes about as a
shadow. . . .*

*Man heaps up and knows not who
will gather!
And now, Lord, for what do I wait?
My hope is in thee.*

Psalm 39:4-7

**The life of every Christian is
dominated by uneasiness — he
cannot escape from God.**

Dietrich Bonhoeffer

Give Me the Strength to Go On Hoping

**The greatest miracle of your grace,
Lord, is that we have hope. However
much unhappiness, failure, and
suffering we see around us, we go on
hoping that things will be better.**

**I thank you, Lord, that I can still
hope, despite everything that I have
experienced. I cannot rely on what I
possess now. I can only live for what is
still to come. I live for the future.**

**Lord, give me the strength to go on
hoping In spite of all the evil that I see**

around me. Give me unshakeable confidence in your love. You are stronger than man's weakness and lack of resolution. You always keep your promise. Let me be happy, then, Lord, because I hope.

I thank you that I can be patient in distressing circumstances. I am glad that I can go on praying.

Life is meaningful if we have brought a little more goodness and love or a little more light and truth into the world.

Alfred Delp

As the End Approaches

As the end approaches, Lord, increase my understanding and make my heart more open. I want to be ready for that great moment when you take me into the fullness of life and make me happy forever.

And the World passes away and the lust of it, but he who does the will of God abides forever.

1 John 2:17

What is a man's life? Add as many years to it as you will and prolong the evening of your life; it still gets shorter every moment.

St. Augustine

Today, many people will die. As a result of this, many other people will be very sad. This is the way we all must follow.

Give us the grace to make this last, decisive step worthily. Let it be a happy step toward you.

What sense is there in devoting all our attention to things that we shall certainly have to leave behind? Surely it is much more sensible to give our love to what will remain forever.

Leo the Great

VII. In the Evening

The Best Time of Day

We have all spent bad nights that we shall never forget — nights of anxiety, sorrow, or fear (think of the war!), nights when we could not sleep because we were so wretched. But God made the night out of kindness to us. He wanted to give us quietness and peace. That is why we always say to each other: Good night.

But how often this wish is made a lie by people. Darkness is used as a cloak for sin, theft, violence, or murder.... And so many nights are spent in tears or self-reproach.... When you are old, this often happens when you are lying awake, unable to sleep.

But we know that nighttime is good. It is holy. The night when the angels sang: Peace on earth! Nicodemus came to talk with Jesus in the night.... The Last Supper took place at night.... Easter night — the holiest of all!

Our nights are often blessed and we often feel secure at night. Some people get up every night to pray for us. Others work every night so that we can sleep safely. We must trust the night. Jesus protects the night. Angels watch over us. The ancient Christian practice of sanctifying by prayer the time when day becomes night was good.

Now that we are old, we need more time to get to sleep. That is not in itself bad. It can be a source of light and wisdom. . . . The evening is the most peaceful and often the most fruitful time of day. It is the time for sincere understanding. It is often a great gift. Our heart is made more gentle. Our senses are at rest. We do not have to exert ourselves so much. A different light is shed on our problems and cares. We see everything in a more gentle and benevolent light.

The evening may be the best time of all in the life of those of us who are getting older.

Robert Svoboda

Thank You for Every Day

Before I go to bed, Lord, I want to thank you for all the good things that have happened in my life today.

I thank you that I have been able to do a few things and that the day has been well spent. You have given me the chance to do good to others and perhaps to make them happy. I thank you for that. Everything I have done has come from you.

I ask you to forgive me for everything that I have done wrong. You do not want sinners to die; you want them to turn back to you and live. So I turn to you, Lord. Let me please you in my life.

I want to do your will, because I am thankful that you are always coming forward to meet me and are always aware of what I really need. I dedicate myself to you, because you are always with me and want me to be happy. I place my trust in you, because I can always be secure in your arms.

I want to look forward happily to every new day — your gift — and to all the good things that you will give me every tomorrow of my life, because you are always so close to me. One day, the tomorrow will last forever.

Being a Christian consists nowadays of two things: prayer and just behavior toward our fellow men. Everything we think, do or organize in Christianity must be tested against our prayer and behavior.

Dietrich Bonhoeffer

I Entrust Myself to You

Lord, you have given me so much today. You have been with me all day. You have shown me your way and have protected me from misfortune. You have been merciful to me in my weakness and have helped me in everything. I thank you, Lord, for being my Father.

Forgive me, Lord, for neglecting prayer and work, for being without love sometimes, for giving too little attention to others, and for not being entirely sincere in my words and actions. Give me strength and the good will to follow the way that you show me. You are the end of that way, the fulfillment of my life.

I entrust myself to you. I lie down to sleep without any cares and give myself entirely to you: my whole life, all my thoughts and deeds, and everything that troubles me. You have blessed me today and I am very thankful. I know that you will also bless me tomorrow.

It is only because we have hope that we are always ready to begin again.

Charles Péguy

The truth is that, as soon as we no longer have to work in order to support ourselves, we no longer know what to do with our lives. There is a great danger then of wasting our lives.

André Gide

I Come Home to You

Lord, I come home to you
as I come home to myself.
I offer you everything —
the joys of this day,
the sorrows and the sufferings,
all that is good
and all that is bad.

I give myself to you as I am.
If you ask me how I am,
I must reply that my heart
is not yet pure,
not yet hammered and forged
in your image,
but as I am, I am for you.

Help me, Lord, to carry on.
Time is passing.
Help me on, O Lord.
Today is over.
Let me be better tomorrow.

Ignaz Klug

**The greatest obstacle to becoming
really holy Christians is that we do not**

reflect enough. We do not look inward and do not know what we are doing. What we need most of all is to reflect and then, through prayer, to come into contact with God.

Curé d'Ars

Becoming more mature means making clearer distinctions and firmer connections.

Hugo von Hofmannsthal

I was old and my hair was white
and I was stiff and tired,
waiting in the old house
where despair had often come
and filled me with fear
until I sweated all over.
  How often I looked out
to see if Jesus was coming!
  But, O wise Lord!
you may come soon
or you may be slow in coming —
Your name be praised!
You will come at the proper time.

Jan Luiken

Thank You for Everything

I thank you, Lord, for the food that I eat every day. I thank you for all those who take care that we have what we need. I thank you too for all the spiritual food that I receive — the kind words and the comfort others give me. I thank you for the love of other people, the friendship they show me in word and deed. I thank you, Lord, that you are so close to us and care for us like a father.

Give Me Your Blessing

Lord, at the end of this day I thank you for all the good things you have given me in your love.

I thank you too for all the good things that you have given me through other people: all the friendly glances, all the encouraging words, all the good deeds — everything I have received from others that has made this day so good.

I admit that I have been very negligent today, because of weakness or inattentiveness or because I have wanted things for myself. Forgive me for all that I have done wrong and help me put it right.

Give me your blessing and bless those who are dear to me, the members of my family, my friends and acquaintances, all who are sick or unhappy, all who are lonely or in despair, and all who are dying or already dead.

Give us all your peace.

The only thing that can really help us overcome the petty difficulties of everyday life, as well as those that seem to be much more important, is faith. The only thing that can keep our souls fixed on higher things — things of real importance, — is faith.

Wilhelm von Humboldt

It is astonishing how clever people can be in their attempts to avoid making a final decision.

Sören Kierkegaard

I am waiting for you
as I wait in the morning
after a sad and sleepless night.
Life cannot always be so dark,
so empty and so comfortless.

I know that you are there —
full of love and forgiveness,
full of strength and understanding.
You are stronger than the night and
confusion,
stronger than our guilt and shortcomings.

For you are all light
and you banish our darkness.
You are all mercy
and you take away our guilt.
You are all love
and you fill our empty existence.

Séverin Schneider

You Are Always with Me

*O Lord, thou hast searched me and
known me!*
Thou knowest when I sit down and

when I rise up.
Thou discernest my thoughts from afar.
Thou searchest out my path and my lying down,
*   and art acquainted with all my ways.*
Even before a word is on my tongue,
*   lo, O Lord, thou knowest it altogether.*
Thou dost beset me behind and before,
*   and layest thy hand upon me.*
Such knowledge is too wonderful for me;
*   so high that I cannot attain it.*

Whither shall I go from thy Spirit?
Or whither shall I flee from thy presence?
If I ascend to heaven, thou art there!
If I make my bed in Sheol, thou art there!
If I take the wings of the morning
*   and dwell in the uttermost parts of the sea,*
*   even there thy hand shall lead me,*
*   and thy right hand shall hold me.*
If I say, "Let only darkness cover me.
*   and the light about me be night,"*
*   even the darkness is not dark to thee.*

The night is as bright as the day,
for darkness is as light with thee.

For thou didst form my inward parts,
thou didst knit me together in my
mother's womb.
I praise thee, for thou art fearful and
wonderful.
Wonderful are thy works!

Psalm 136:1-14

I Am Alone with You

The world is sleeping. I am alone with you as you watch over everything.

I thank you for having taken such care of me and for protecting me today. I thank you too for all the comfort and help I have received from the good people you let me meet. The day has been full of good things, and I have your love to thank for that.

But I ask you to forgive me for the ways in which I have fallen short today. I ask you, too, to make up for my shortcomings with your love. My intention was good, but I lacked the strength to do what I should have done.

Give me a quiet night so that I can rest and gain strength for the following day. Bless all those who are ill or in pain. Be close to us. Be our Savior. Give us hope. Make our lives full. Let us, Lord, always have people around us who will help us.

When I wake up tomorrow morning, let me be happy in the knowledge that I can look forward to your nearness. Let me be conscious that each day brings me a little nearer to my end — to you. You are all in all for me.

The nights are often very lonely, but that is why they are not too difficult. Sometimes a great deal occurs at nighttime: we draw up the balance sheet of our life, and even of the whole world, which we, with others, have made. The more we think about it, the more severe our judgment is bound to be.

Reinhold Schneider

Every day brings new life. We have the chance to make up for our mistakes of the previous day.

Alban Stolz

When you call me to work for you,
   before I take off my wornout dress,
I pray that you will never forget me,
   or dismiss me before the end of the day.

Lord, I am weaker than I used to be,
   more easily discouraged and afraid.
My body has gathered so much fatigue
   and the task of life is more demanding.

I would like to rest, but know
   I may not until you say I can:
   that my work is over and my service done.
So I pray: Pour once more through my blood
   a little of your fire of love
   and once again support my limbs with strength.

Henriette Roland Holst

With Your Blessing, I Go to Rest

The evening is familiar to me; I have experienced it many times. But now it points to the end of my life. Every time evening approaches, I know that a little more of my life has passed. Yet everything that I have done, and still do, is to some extent of lasting value, both the good things and those less good. You will reward the good I have done with your blessing and consider what is less good by your mercy.

You have given me the will to serve you, and that is good, but you know how weak I am and how difficult I find it to respond when you urge me to do good. So I ask you to forgive me for everything that I have done that is not good and for the many times that I have failed to love you.

You have always been good to me and I know you always will be. That is why I dare to ask you for the strength to do better tomorrow.

With your blessing, I go to rest, trusting in your love. The time will come when I shall go to rest forever.

Help me, therefore, to live in preparation for that great encounter with you. Then I shall find perfect rest in you, my God and my all.

It is foolish to lie awake at night, full of care and anxiety. Your problems will not be solved, and in the morning you will be less able to cope with the day.

In life, one must learn to be thankful for even the smallest things. Then everything will be easier and clearer.

Friedrich von Bodelschwingh

Lord, Stay with Us

Stay with us, Lord,
for evening is approaching
and the day is drawing to a close.

Stay with us
and with your Church.

Stay with us
in the evening of this day,

the evening of our life,
the evening of the world.

Stay with us
with your grace and goodness,
with your word and sacrament,
with your comfort and blessing.

Stay with us
as night comes down on us,
the night of care and anxiety,
the night of doubt and struggle,
the night of bitter death.

Stay with us,
with all who believe in you —
stay with us now and in eternity.